FROM
RESUME
TO WORK

FROM RESUME TO WORK

How to get your resume to help you find
a job faster than it has ever done before.

C. Edwin Gill

From Resume to Work

ISBN: 1519547633 / ISBN-13: 978-1519547637

Please note that throughout this book I use URL shorteners from Bit.do (**http://bit.do**) which makes it easier for you to type in a link that I reference in this book instead of having to type in the full link which often is very long. You will see URL shorteners displayed like this: **/FRTW38.** This means for you to type in **http://bit.do/FRTW38** in the URL bar to bring up the site.

Who this book is for...

From Resume to Work was written with one goal in mind: to show you how to get your resume to connect with the employer so that he or she contacts you for an interview so that you can get the job that you want. This book is for everyone who wants to work.

This book is for the employee who has had a job for a period of time, who is about to be laid off, and is nervous about reentering the job market. *From Resume to Work* will help you by exposing some of the psychology employers use today to judge you based upon your resume and will help you to avoid this negative psychology.

This book is for the job seeker who has recently entered the workforce and may have little or no experience and wonder how they can get the skills if they don't have a job in the first place. *From Resume to Work* will explain the techniques that others have used to get a job when their work history is scattered at best.

This book is for the job applicant who has a job posting in mind but has been out of work for quite some time and lacks confidence in applying for the position. *From Resume to Work* will share with you techniques that anyone can use to connect with the employer no matter how long they have been out of the job market.

This book is also for every employer who agonizes over the hiring process and wants to find the best candidate as quickly as possible. Although this book was written with the applicant in mind, employers have gained a wealth of information from this book that they now use with every hire.

It is my sincere desire that you would use this book and that this book would work for you in order to move you *From Resume to Work*.

Thank you.

C. Edwin Gill

p.s. Be sure to visit our blog at **www.GudeJob.com** where we promote on the job success in many areas in life that you didn't know you already had a job.

Your Free Gift

In my book, *From Resume to Work,* I share with you the 10 challenges to watch out for on your resume and how employers are now looking at each challenge as a potential landmine in your business character which gives them another reason to pass on your resume. I then share a pet peeve of the most anal of employers called the *dangling* resume.

As a way of saying *thank you* for your purchase I would like to offer you a free compliment to this book called *5 Fixes to the Dangling Resume.*

5 Fixes to the Dangling Resume provides you with five ways to correct the dangling resume thereby saving you from getting passed over for that particular landmine. It is a part of my developing Solutions Series in which I share step-by-step solutions to a particular issue.

Your free gift comes as a PDF download. It is a resource of over 25 pages that includes detailed steps along with screenshots of how to fix your dangling resume problem. I again want to thank you for your purchase.

Simply go to **FromResumeToWork.com** to get your free gift today.

Table of Contents

Checklists Before Getting Started 87

Resources 91

Next Steps 111
Thank You 113

INTRODUCTION

You have your resume in hand and you're looking for work, so what do you do? Send it out to potential employers, right? True, but before you do you may want to know that this book, *From Resume to Work*, has some extremely important experiences to share with you to help your resume put you to work faster than it has ever done before.

My goal is show you how to get the employer to absolutely, positively, and undeniably fall in love with your resume every time by making the right connection with him or her.

After you read this book, listen to it, and then put into practice the strategies which are sure to move you *From Resume to Work*.

How many resumes should you send out before you get that first response: 10? 20? 100? Recent studies show that unless a person has a specialized skill for a high-demanding job, it usually takes 25 to 50 resumes before you can expect your first response, a two-to-four percent response rate. And by a response we mean that the employer loves your resume and wants to connect with you to follow up about it.

This is not unusual. In today's economy with massive layoffs, a growing workforce, and access through technology, employers are squeezed for time and resources when it comes to searching for candidates. One job posting could yield 100 responses or more, so finding the right person is often like searching for a missing piece to a huge jigsaw puzzle. Your job (and mine) is to make it easier for the employer to select your resume above all others.

You Have The Advantage

Using this book gives you an advantage over every other job seeker who does not have this resource. It was developed with the assistance and input from human resource professionals, job developers, hiring managers, head hunters, employment psychologists, employment agencies, business owners, non-profit professionals, and managers in government with over 40 years' experience of hiring people across multiple industries. Many of these professionals continue to stay on the cutting edge of hiring practices and trends in the marketplace.

In addition, portions of this material were developed for use in job workshops and seminars where employers were instructed on effective methods of hiring the right person. In short, you have a powerful tool that when used correctly will yield a definite increase in your resume response rate.

Taking Some First Steps

The first step in preparing to use this material is to make sure that you have your resume and cover letter up to date. Produce what you will use as your finished product and make sure that you are satisfied that it is polished and ready to send out. It is always best to have another set of eyes look at your resume. Even if writing resumes is your thing, it is important to get as much constructive feedback as possible.

Once your resume and cover letter are completed and ready to go, write *TEMPLATE* on them. That's right. What you thought was your final, finished product serves only as your template for the purposes of this book. 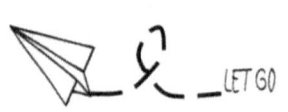 Remember that no resume is ever static if you want to increase your resume response rate and make the transition from resume to work. Therefore, your second step is to let go of the notion that a single version of your resume will work for any and every job posting.

The third step in using this material is that you must prepare yourself to slow down your resume campaign. This may mean applying for fewer positions than you have in the past. This notion is contrary to the job hunting method that too many job seekers are relying on today: *the blasting method.*

The blasting method is where you send out a standard resume and cover letter to practically any and every job posting that even faintly resembles what you might want to do for work. This method has increased over the years as more people enter or re-enter the workforce, and continues to be used more often as the time it takes to find a job increases from weeks to months to years.

Employers now are getting more savvy to blasters and will pass over their resume for one that employs the strategies outlined in *From Resume to Work* because blasters are now being seen as desperate, inconsiderate, lacking attention to detail, and impersonal, among other things. Remember that employers are looking to make a connection with their next employee when sifting through resumes. Another downside to blasting is that you may eventually get a response to your resume for a job you have to settle for rather than the job that you really want.

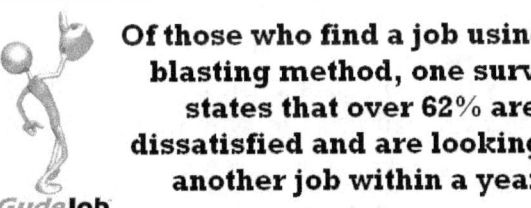

Of those who find a job using the blasting method, one survey states that over 62% are dissatisfied and are looking for another job within a year.

GudeJob

So when going through this material understand that your finished resume is just the starting point, that no single resume will work for any and every job, and that blasting your standard resume and cover letter is not the cure-all to finding the job you really want.

However, I realize that some of you reading this book need help building your resume and cover letter. I have provided some resources at the end of this book to help you get started creating the finished resume you desire.

What You Can Expect

As you implement the techniques outlined throughout this book you will not only understand why your resume had such a low response rate, but you will also begin to experience an increase in employers desiring to connect with you because of how you are now connecting with them. The strategies in *From Resume to Work* have made a success story out of many job-seekers, and the same can be done for you too.

From Resume to Work covers the three essential areas needed to increase your resume response rate: (1) understanding why resumes get rejected, (2) knowing how to answer the employer's questions before they ask, and (3) finding the best ways to connect with the employer.

Why DO resumes get rejected? First of all, you may think you know why your resume is not connecting with the employer, but there is a growing trend among employers and employment agencies that have been fueled by psychologists in the employment industry. This trend offers some explanation as to why more and more resumes are being rejected.

If you do a Google search on human resources and psychology you will find links that show how psychologists are now more involved in employee screening, as in the example below.

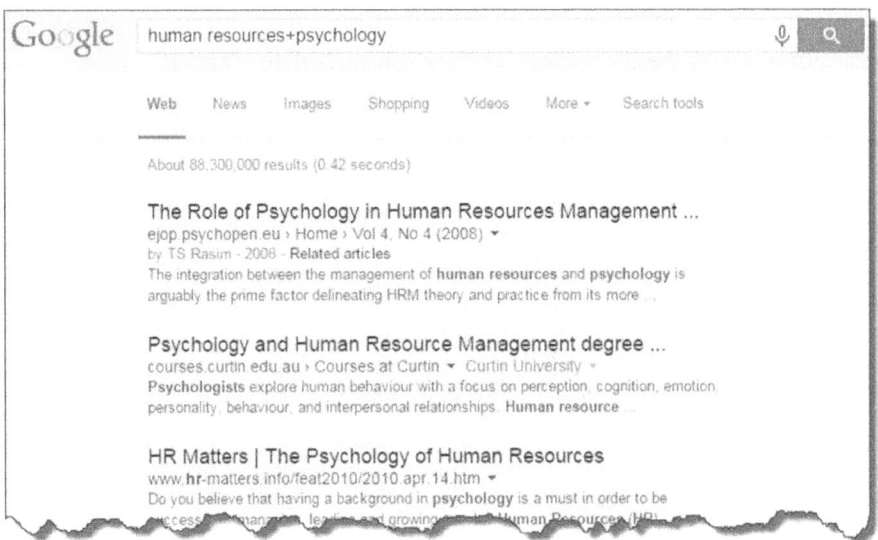

From Resume to Work helps you, first of all, to avoid the pitfalls that these employment psychologists have created for the applicant by sharing with you what they are saying to employers about your resume.

Second, *From Resume to Work* helps you to answer one of the top questions on the employer's mind before they ask it: *What are you doing now?* This is key because an employer would prefer to not make the effort to contact you and ask what you are currently doing and instead go on to someone who has already answered that question for them. There remains a stigma against the unemployed that unfortunately remains today (**/FRTW37**):

> In a 2012 study, three researchers from UCLA and one from the State University of New York at Stony Brook found a hiring bias exists against applicants as soon as they're unemployed and only gets worse the longer they are out of work.
>
> Another, conducted last year by Northeastern University researcher Rand Ghayad, found the bias was more severe the longer an applicant was jobless. He found the long-term unemployed had to send out 3.5 times as many resumes as the short-term unemployed just to get an interview.

"It's a stigma," said Ian Calderon, a Democrat who sponsored the Assembly legislation in California. "If you're unemployed, there's an attitude they feel they face (from employers) of 'If nobody else wants you, why should I want you?'"

This material shows you ways you can always answer the question of what you are doing now in the workforce regardless of your present situation.

Third, this guide explains the number one principle you need to get your resume responded to that over 95% of job seekers are not using today. This is the principle of connecting with the employer. Most people think that unless you know the employer or are referred to them by a friend, you really don't have a chance to make a connection with them. This is not true! *From Resume to Work* will show you the motivation behind the job posting and lead you through strategies you need to make that connection with the employer.

After covering the three essential areas to increase your resume response rate, you are provided with checklists that you can print out and use before applying for each job. It is our goal for you to begin to see job postings from the perspective of the employer and know how to respond to them so that they will respond to you. In other words, move you *From Resume to Work*.

Introduction Points

Point 1: Unless you have specialized skills for a specialized job, don't be surprised if you have about a two-to-four percent response rate from your resume submissions.

Point 2: This book walks you through the process of making it easier for the employer to respond to your resume.

Point 3: Your finished resume and cover letter are just the starting point for the purposes of this book.

Point 4: Do not expect a single resume to work for any and every job posting.

Point 5: Relying on the blasting method is not the cure-all to finding the job you really want.

Point 6: This book helps you in three areas: identifying why resumes get rejected, answering the employer's question about what you are doing now, and showing you how to connect with the employer.

Point 7: When you implement *From Resume to Work* strategies, expect to increase your resume response rate.

RESUMES THAT GET REJECTED

After you have worked hard to develop a perfect resume you send it out and don't hear anything back. Why is that? Has your resume been received? Was it lost in cyberspace? Was the recipient on vacation? Probably not. Not hearing back from a resume submission is usually a clear sign that it was rejected.

No one likes rejection, especially when it comes to their resume, the essence of their entire educational and working life boiled down to one piece of paper. So why was *your* resume rejected? Resumes are rejected for a variety of reasons, but primarily fall into one or more of the five rejection categories which can be called *The Five Not's*:

One: Not Following Instructions

Two: Not Correcting a Challenging Resume

Three: Not Checking the Resume (and Cover Letter) Again

Four: Not Meeting Minimum Qualifications

Five: Not Being Present

1. Not Following Instructions

A large number of job-seekers are unaware that there is a growing trend among employers to "test" applicants before they even submit their resume. This trend has been fueled by employment psychologists who are helping employers find the right candidate as efficiently as possible.

Employers are being trained to give a few simple instructions in their job postings to candidates, usually in the "How To Apply" section of the posting. If the candidate follows the instructions exactly as it is outlined in the "How To Apply" section, employers are urged to move this candidate to the top of the interview list as it has a tendency to mean that the applicant pays attention to detail, has a higher level of perception, and knows how to follow instructions. In fact, one employer reported that for a company job posting only 4 out of 37 applicants followed the instructions on the job posting, so he only interviewed those four without even looking at the other resumes. And, he hired one of the interviewees.

One employer gave applicants a number pattern (abcd1234efgh5678) and told them to write the last four letters of this pattern on their resume. He reported that of the 28% who attempted his instructions only 62% got it right.

*Gude*Job

In my recent experience I needed someone to quickly cut the high grass on some property I own in another city before I was fined, so I placed an ad in Craigslist specifically stating that along with the grass cut bid I needed photos of the property to be sent to me to show that they knew the scope of the job. Eighteen people responded to my ad and sent me bids, but only one sent the requested photos. His bid was $75, and even though I had seven bids lower than his, I hired this guy who sent the photos because I knew he could follow instructions.

If a candidate does not follow the instructions given in an ad, employment psychologists urge the employer to reject the resume no matter how good it looks because this candidate might be dull, self-absorbed, or even arrogant. At the very least the candidate does not follow instructions well and does not pay attention to detail.

For example, the illustration below is an actual job posting for a Facilities Manager for a Lutheran Church. In the second section the applicant is given specific instructions to email their one-page cover letter and resume, send two professional references, and make sure that the job title, "Facilities Manager," is in the subject line.

Facilities Manager (cupertino)

About: Bethel Lutheran Church and School has served the South Bay for more than 50 years through ministries for children and youth, adults, and seniors. Planted in the heart of Silicon Valley, the Bethel community seeks to grow in relationship to God and to all people through worship, study, and service to neighbors both near and far. Bethel Lutheran School's mission is to actively engage students in a strong academic and enrichment curriculum with the goal of developing the fundamental skills and unique talents of each student. Bethel is currently seeking a Facilities Manger to join our team.

To Apply: Please email a one-page cover letter and resume, highlighting relevant skills and background for the position to mnadell@bethells.org with "Facilities Manager" in the subject line. Please provide two professional references. Submissions without cover letter or references will not be considered. Due to the volume of applications, we regret that we cannot respond to each individual applicant. No phone calls please.

Classification: Full-Time, Benefited, Exempt Position

In the past, employers would still review resumes that did not necessarily follow each instruction; however, employers today are encouraged to reject resumes of candidates who do not dot their *i*'s and cross their *t*'s.

Question: Would you try to contact the employer above by phone if you saw their number in the job ad? *Answer*: Absolutely not. In the "To Apply" section the employer specifically asks not to contact them by phone. Some employers give similar instructions and do, perhaps inadvertently, list their phone number. If a job applicant calls anyway employment psychologists have urged employers to put them on the "Do Not Hire" list. (Even so, there has been at least one case where the employer did ask candidates not to call but did place their phone number in the job posting. It was a sales job, and the candidate who called anyway got the job for being persistent. But this is the exception rather than the norm.)

This point is important enough to recap. For the above *Facilities Manager* posting you would want to follow the employer's instructions by:

a. Emailing a 1-page cover letter.
b. Emailing a 1-page resume (even if your resume is two pages you must follow instructions and shrink it down to one for this posting.
c. Highlight your relevant skills and background (usually in the cover letter or in the Summary section of your resume).
d. Be sure to email it to the correct person.
e. Be sure that "Facilities Manager" is in the subject line of your email.
f. Provide two professional references, generally in the cover letter but almost never on your resume. Make sure to provide only two professional references.
g. Do not call them about the position or the status of your resume. It is still okay to send a follow-up email regarding the position.

Unfortunately, all too many applicants will not follow instructions and take the directives above as suggestions only to find out that once again their resume is passed over for an applicant who knows how to follow instructions.

So you the applicant must now pay special attention to any job posting that requests you to do specific tasks. It is, more than likely, a test to screen out applicants.

2. Not Correcting a Challenging Resume

When an employer receives your resume the first thing they look for is whether or not the resume is challenging; i.e., is it aesthetically pleasing to their eyes? Is the font large enough? Is the font too large? Is it crooked? Is there something missing? Can I see everything on one, or at most, two pages? Is it inviting? If the resume is challenging, if their first impression is that something is wrong, then there is a very high probability that it will be rejected on the first or second pass.

A challenging resume has two types of challenges: first, the challenge *on* the resume—on the face of it, what it looks like, or how it is formatted. Then there is a challenge *in* the resume—whether or not what is said conveys and coincides with what the employer is looking for in a job applicant.

Employers reject 84% of resumes on the first pass when they consider the resume "challenging." How challenging is your resume?

GudeJob

Challenges on your resume can be easily fixed using the techniques outline in this book. It is as simple as identifying the challenge and then correcting it. Challenges in your resume can be much harder to fix. Some of the most common challenges in the resume include:

a) Missing requirements.
b) No degree, or only a little college experience.
c) Over-qualified for a job; also under-qualified.
d) Too much job-hopping.
e) Gaps in your work history being too far apart.
f) Too old, or too young.
g) Cultural identity (like your name, or where you are from).

Each challenge in your resume has to be addressed in its own particular way and is why many people seek out some type of professional resume writing help. I have therefore included a number of resources at the end of this book that I hope that you will find helpful in correcting challenges in your resume.

However, the employer may never get to the challenges in your resume if they are consumed by the challenges on your resume. Employment psychologists have earned their keep by giving employers a psychology behind challenges on resumes and point out that each challenge may mask a trait about the applicant that the employer should seriously consider before selecting a candidate.

An example of a challenging resume is illustrated below. On this resume are ten of the most common challenges that these employment psychologists are instructing employers to watch out for. If your resume is guilty of any one of these challenges it could be the reason why the employer hasn't connected with you as a serious candidate for employment:

Eric Flowers 1
7613 – 15th Street, Oakland, CA 94621
(510) 776-4309 2
stupidme23@oakmail.com 3

Summary
· Demonstrated achiever with exceptional knowledge of international markets, business practices, and trade regulations.
· Strong marketing and finance background combined with fluency in several languages, including "Advanced Level" U. 4
S. State Department certification in Russian Language Reading Comprehension.
5 Enthusiastic and experienced in overseas travel.

6

Education Masters Degree in Russian & East European Studies *2014*
Oak Tree University, Washington, D.C.

B.A. Degree in Foreign Languages *2012*
7 *Elm College, Coral Gables, FL*
Concentration in Russian, Spanish, French, & Italian; graduated cum laude with 3.8 G.P.A.

Career History & Accomplishments

Assistant to the Director of Business Development, *Fabrikam, Inc.* *2012-2015*
· Worked directly with Director of Business Development and
8 Director of Strategic planning of this large, publicly-traded provider of home healthcare services.
9 ·
· Researched and wrote marketing, financial, and feasibility reports concerning new business acquisitions and acquisition prospects.
· Prepared corporate financial reports and service contracts for the CFO.

Memberships & Affiliations
· Founding member of the Former Soviet Union Florida Chamber of Commerce
· Member, American Association for Advancement of Slavic Studies
· Member, World Affairs Council

10

---

1) *The name does not stand out.* If your name is small and unassuming an employer might not remember your name or your resume. Psychologists tell employers that unassuming candidates may have low self-esteem issues or may be trying to hide something about a negative personality trait. Be sure to make your name stand out at least a little by making the font size larger than the rest of the text or changing the font style.

What is the best font size for your name? If you are using an easy-to-read font such as Times New Roman, Arial, Verdana, Palatino, or Geneva; and, the body of your resume is between the standard 10 point and 12 point, a good range for your name should be between 16 and 22 points. Your name should also be in bold so that it stands out and makes an impression on the resume reviewer.

2) *Minimal or unidentified phone contact.* In this case there is only one phone number with no reference to it. Employers are told that the more contact information the applicant provides the more stable the candidate tends to be. If your only phone contact is not labeled the employer may hesitate contacting you (at least by phone) because they do not have a clue how the number connects to you. You should list your cell phone number, a home phone number, and (believe it or not) a personal fax number, if possible. And always identify the numbers that you provide.

If you need to add more numbers to your resume you could add a free voicemail or free fax number. Although the recommended free voicemail services I shared for years no longer offers voicemail, you can still use **Google Voice** to get a number if someone would allow you to set it up using their phone. Once you sign up Google will give you your own phone number where you can use your computer to access your voicemail messages.

You can also receive a free fax number from services such as **Faxbetter.com** which gives you a dedicated toll free fax number that you can include on your resume. However, you can only keep the free fax number as long as you use the fax number given every seven days as of the writing of this material.

3) *Use of a crazy email address.* Your email address says a lot about you to an employer. Employment psychologists warn employers that candidates that use an email address with a handle like stupidme23 or dawg4life or anything alluding to profanity is an indication of how the candidate could tarnish the reputation of the employer and the company. Get another email address. The most powerful type of email address is one where you would use your full name such as **billsmith@mymail.com**. The Top 10 free email services (and links to them or URL shortened links) are listed below (remember when you see the reference such as /FRTW41, this means to type in the shortener link http://bit.do/FRTW41 in the URL bar):

1) **Google Mail** (/FRTW41)
2) **Yahoo Mail** (/FRTW42)
3) **Outlook Mail** (www.Outlook.com)
4) **Zoho Mail** (www.Zoho.com/mail)
5) **Yandex Mail** (www.mail.Yandex.com)
6) **AOL Mail** (www.aol.com)
7) **iCloud Mail** (www.Apple.com/icloud)
8) **Mail.com and GMX Mail** (www.gmx.com)
9) **Inbox.com Mail** (www.inbox.com)
10) **Juno.com** (www.juno.com/freeemail)

You don't have to use the most popular free email accounts (like Gmail). As long as you have your full name as an email account you can use any email service which suits you. Some people simply go down the list to find which one can accommodate their full name.

4) *Non-uniform paragraphs.* Paragraphs are supposed to run to the end of the page so that they would not leave an empty feeling in the minds of employers that something is missing. Employers at a number of training workshops I participated in shared with us that against their better judgment they have interviewed and hired candidates in the past who left holes in paragraphs only to discover later that their suspicions were confirmed.

Psychologists tell employers not to ignore this feeling and to pass on the resume. Make sure that your paragraphs fill up the section appropriately. In Microsoft Word one method is to use the Show/Hide (¶) button to make sure that you did not accidently split a paragraph as illustrated below.

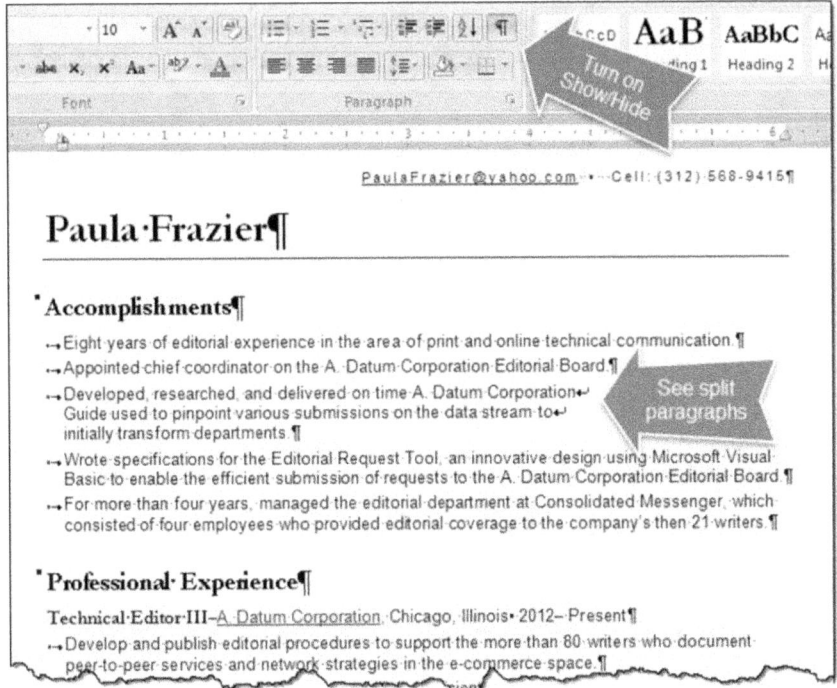

5) *Missing Bullet Points.* Leaving a bullet point missing can send a signal to the employer that your technical skills may be lacking. Employers are instructed to look for inconsistencies in a person's resume where their **Skills** section says they are proficient in Microsoft Word but then they leave out something as small as a bullet point in a paragraph. Psychologists say that inconsistencies such as these may reveal that the candidate is careless with the truth or just plain careless. Take a moment to highlight the section where you want the bullet points and turn the **Bullets** tool on so that each paragraph is bulleted as illustrated below.

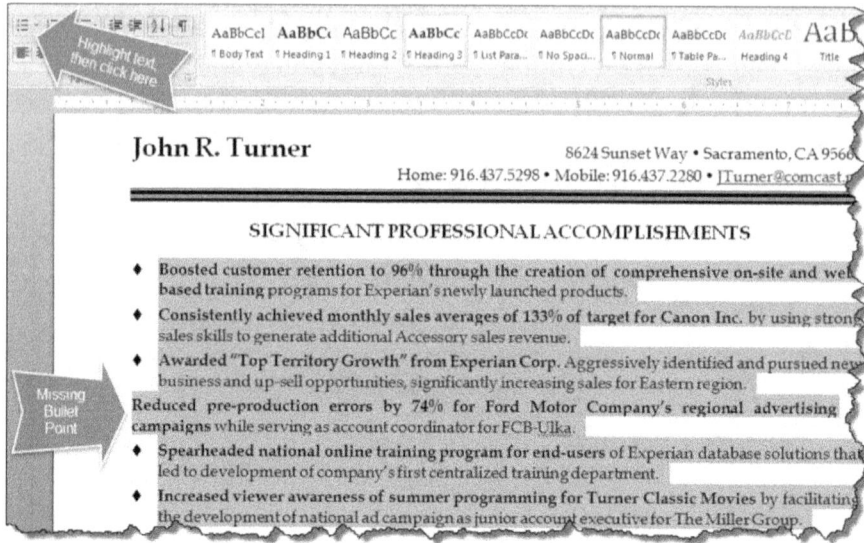

6) *Use of extra spaces.* Using extra spaces purposely or accidently causes the employer to think that you are trying to pad your resume to make yourself look like you have more to offer than you really do. Psychologists tell employers to give resumes with extra spacing more scrutiny, especially when doing employment and educational background checks. Spacing should be consistent and the maximum spacing between paragraphs should be a single line space.

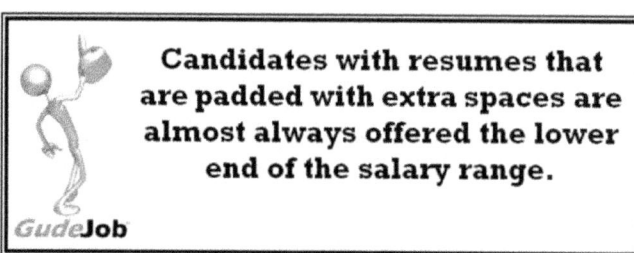

Candidates with resumes that are padded with extra spaces are almost always offered the lower end of the salary range.

GudeJob

7) *Inconsistent indentation.* When the alignments of your paragraph are not consistent the employer now wonders if inconsistencies on your resume are a reflection of an underlying inconsistent work pattern. Why would you find it perfectly acceptable to indent one line but not indent the other? Unfortunately, employment psychologists have asserted to employers that this type of inconsistent display could suggest that the candidate has a mild form of schizophrenia.

Although these psychologists point out that this is no reason to reject an applicant outright, the employer must be aware that they should not consider applicants for positions requiring attention to detail. Employers who especially need someone to write reports are warned by employment psychologists to look out for these types of inconsistencies on a resume. Make sure that if you indent one paragraph you indent them all.

8) *Inconsistent Font usage.* This sends a signal to the employer that you might not have worked on your resume yourself. Even though this is ok in general, you have the overall responsibility for your resume being perfect and submitting a resume with varying font usage fuels the psychologist's suggestion to the employer that you might be someone who allows stuff to fall through the cracks. To make sure that you don't receive this label you could highlight your entire resume (Ctrl+A) and choose one font. If you use a second font on your resume be sure that you use it consistently throughout your resume (i.e., your titles or subcategories).

9) *The Lonely Bullet Point.* Employers agree with employment psychologists that this is just plain laziness. Why would a bullet point ever want to be all alone on your resume? Either delete the blank bullet point or add in the appropriate content for it, but never leave it alone on your resume, or the employer might leave you and your resume alone.

10) *A short resume.* Employment psychologists tell employers that if a candidate cannot say enough about himself or herself to fill up at least one page of their resume then they have lived a shallow life, have very little real business experience, or may be running from the law. Always make sure that you say enough about yourself to fill up at least an entire page.

There are a number of places to go if you need resume assistance. You can search Google for *Free Resume Writing Help*, contact a career counseling center at a local college or university, or look for a job placement center at your church or other non-profit organization to help you include pertinent experiences, training, and skills on your resume to fill up an entire page.

 **There were 10 challenges on the resume listed above. Take a moment now to see how many points you can find on your own resume that are challenging.**

GudeJob

In the Resources Section of this book I have included a number of links where you can find resume writing assistance to not only help you with challenges on your resume, but those challenges in your resume. One such resource that I would like to recommend personally and which I am an affiliate of (meaning that if you engage their services then I would receive a referral commission), is the resume writing resource called *Blue Sky Resumes* (go to /FRTW51). Louise Fletcher, the CEO, has helped so many people bring their resumes from zero to hero that I have recommended her for years without question. After Oprah Winfrey had her as a featured expert in the Oprah Winfrey Magazine I knew that more people would begin using her services so I became an affiliate. If you need resume assistance or want expert help doing it yourself, please visit *Blue Sky Resumes* (/FRTW51). Or, check out some of the other resources at the end of this book.

An Employer's Pet Peeve

Another resume issue which is not necessarily considered a "challenge" by employment psychologists, but rather a pet peeve for the more anal employers among us, is the *dangling* resume (see below).

Intake Clerk
- Processed applications for the Urban League Energy Program.
- Collected data from clients to determine eligibility for the program.
- Maintained client files, typed correspondences, and answered telephones.
- Produce monthly reports for all application data processed.

EDUCATION, TRAINING & CERTIFICATION:
- *College Of Lake County*, Grayslake, Illinois (2013). General Education courses.
- *Oakton Community College*, Des Plaines, Illinois (2003-2004). General Education courses.
- *Illinois State University*, Normal, Illinois (1996-1999). Supply Management and Purchasing.
- *Department of the Navy*, San Diego, CA (2011). Simplified Acquisition Procedures coursework.
- *Department of the Navy*, Alameda, CA (2011). Navy Supply Purchase Card Program.
- *Supply and Fiscal Support Management School*, New Orleans, LA (2006).
- *Certificate of Appointment/Contracting Officer*, (February 2012).

JOB-RELATED SKILLS:
- Computer Skills – Microsoft Word, Excel, and Outlook; research over the internet.
- Office and Operational – Calculators, typewriters, forklift (4k, 6k, and 10k).

The dangling resume is a resume which has just a few extra lines of the resume all by themselves on another page. While most employers don't mind having to deal with the few lines of text on another page, a growing number of employers are finding the dangling resume annoying. You should therefore make it a point to do all that you can to eliminate those extra dangling lines on that last page. (To get the free book, *5 Fixes to the Dangling Resume*, visit **www.FromResumeToWork.com** .)

This is the reason why I always recommend sending your resume in PDF format (unless otherwise instructed), so that you can avoid having your resume print out for the employer in a way which you never intended it to look like.

Although you may argue that how employment psychologists interpret challenging resumes does not reflect your character at all, the problem is that once the employer takes note of the psychology associated with resumes it becomes almost impossible for them not to associate your challenging resume with a particular character trait. Unfortunately, your resume would then be rejected. However, employing the techniques in *From Resume to Work* helps you eliminate the challenging resume.

3. Not Checking the Resume (and Cover Letter) Again

Check your resume and cover letter for spelling and grammatical errors. After you finish checking it, check it again. At minimum you should give your resume and cover letter a third pass before sending it out. Be sure to set your resume and cover letter aside for a day or so before the final pass. Employers are offended when they receive a resume and cover letter with spelling or grammatical errors. If a person presents themselves in a careless manner they could represent the company in the same way.

If after you have completed your resume using Microsoft Word you see little squiggly red or squiggly green lines under words (see the illustration below—trust me, these are red and green squiggly lines), that is an indication that you might have spelling or grammatical errors in your resume.

LINDA REINHART   916.437.5289
8526A Sunset Way   916.437.2289 (cell)
Sacramento, CA 95660   lreinhart@comcast.net

QUALIFICATIONS

Highly motibated, customer focused professional with extensive expereince in key client development and retention. Skill in creating and glowing solid customer relationships, needs analysis, account activity tracking.

EXPERIENCE

According to Careerbuilder.com, 61% of resumes containing spelling or grammatical errors will be rejected upon the first pass; and, of those who make it an additional 43% will be disqualified for errors (Adecco.com). Don't just rely on spell check but enlist the help of a friend who knows how to proofread documents. Email your resume to them not only for them to proofread but also so they can see if it prints out as you intended.

If you need an inexpensive alternative to have your resume proofread you can go to *Fiverr* (www.Fiverr.com) and search for "Proofread Resume" in the search section. After that be sure to shop by "High Rating" to find those with the best feedback.

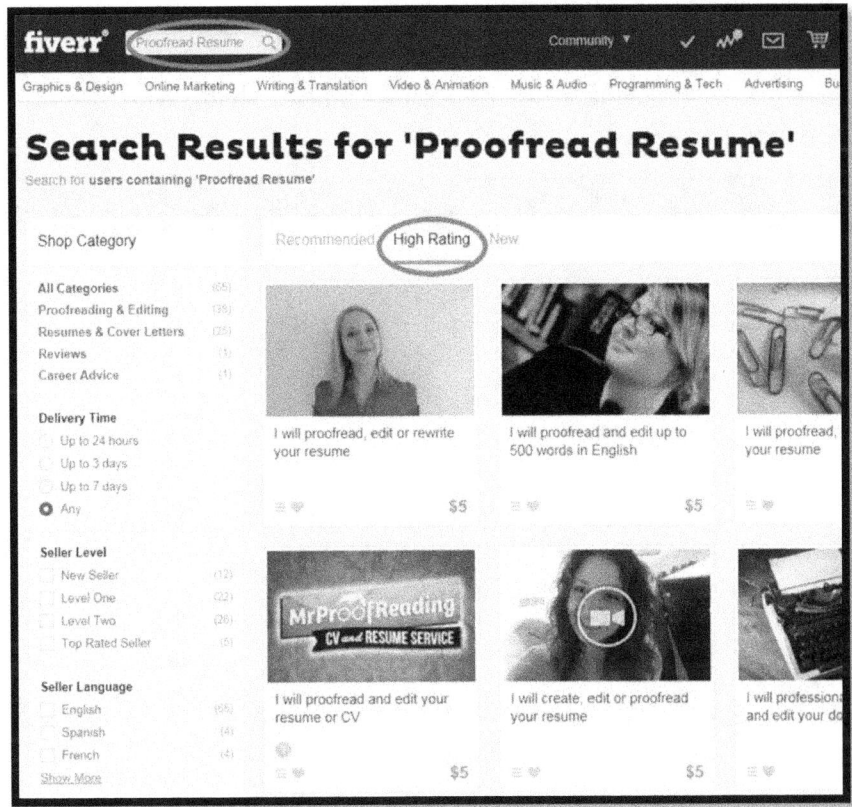

I mentioned this before, but unless you are instructed to send your resume in a certain format, it may be a good idea to create a copy of your resume in PDF format so you know how it will look once the employer receives it and prints it out. Also be sure to title your PDF document as **"YOUR_NAME_Resume"** so the employer can easily identify it.

Another reason to check your resume and cover letter again has to do with identifying inconsistencies between the two. While most people check their resumes and cover letters for spelling and grammatical errors, too many forget to check for consistent information between their resume and cover letter.

For example, if your cover letter (or email) states that you have 10 years' experience as an Account Manager but your resume shows that you only have two, that is an inconsistency that will most likely get your resume booted from the selection process.

This in fact happened to Renita. She sent her email applying for an Account Manager position, where the minimum qualification was 5 years, and stated in an email that she had over 10 years' experience (see below).

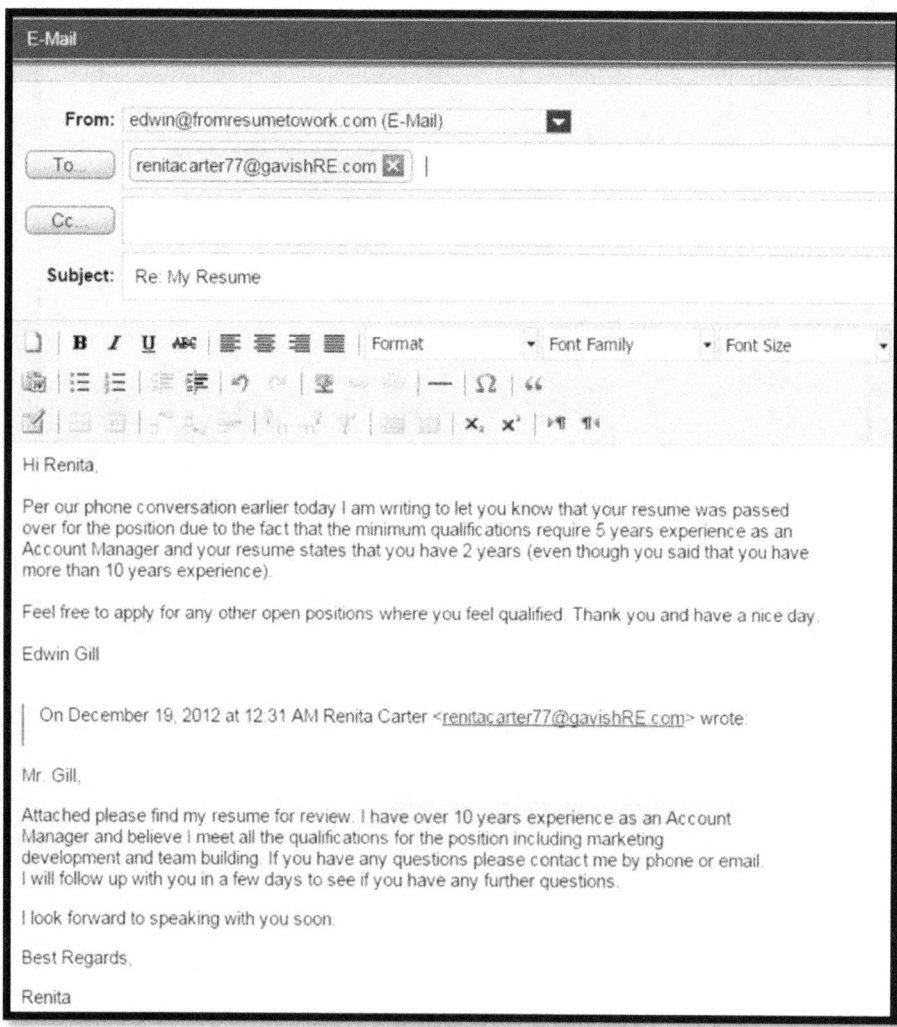

E-Mail

From: edwin@fromresumetowork.com (E-Mail)

To.. renitacarter77@gavishRE.com

Cc..

Subject: Re: My Resume

B *I* U ABC | Format | Font Family | Font Size

Hi Renita,

Per our phone conversation earlier today I am writing to let you know that your resume was passed over for the position due to the fact that the minimum qualifications require 5 years experience as an Account Manager and your resume states that you have 2 years (even though you said that you have more than 10 years experience).

Feel free to apply for any other open positions where you feel qualified. Thank you and have a nice day.

Edwin Gill

On December 19, 2012 at 12:31 AM Renita Carter <renitacarter77@gavishRE.com> wrote:

Mr. Gill,

Attached please find my resume for review. I have over 10 years experience as an Account Manager and believe I meet all the qualifications for the position including marketing development and team building. If you have any questions please contact me by phone or email. I will follow up with you in a few days to see if you have any further questions.

I look forward to speaking with you soon.

Best Regards,

Renita

Renita contacted me a few days later and I told her I would review her resume and send her a response. When I did review her resume I could only find two years' experience as an Account Manager (see below) and had to pass over her resume because she did not meet the minimum qualifications regardless of what her email said. And, because I received over 70 resumes for the position, I wasn't inclined to call her to find out why there was a discrepancy between her email and her resume.

Renita
Carter

6585 High Street
Las Vegas, NV 89113
702.255.1145
renitacarter77@gavishRE.com

SUMMARY OF QUALIFICATIONS

New Business Development

Client Relationship Management

Project Development

PROFESSIONAL EXPERIENCE

GAVISH RE UNLIMITED   Las Vegas, NV
Provider of over 1500 products and services for business form & software solutions.
Account Manager (02/10 – present)
➢ Manage accounts worth 2.5M in annual sales.
➢ Exceeded sales targets in 2008 and 2009 by minimum 50%.
➢ Key player in instigating the company's brand redesign to

Renita contacted me regarding my email response and it turns out that she transposed the year on her resume—it read "02/**10**" but should have been "02/**01**" thereby shaving nine years of needed professional experience off her resume. I felt bad for her and gave her a free copy of *From Resume to Work*. In exchange, she agreed to be the poster child for not checking one's resume over again for the future editions of the book.

Therefore, always do a "fact check" between your resume and cover letter. As the above example illustrates, fact-checking also applies to email responses and your resume. Be sure that whatever you say to an employer via email is consistent with what is stated on your resume because during hiring committee evaluations employers often attach email correspondence to resumes.

4. Not Meeting Minimum Qualifications

When an employer states *Minimum Qualifications* on a job announcement they are sending out a signal that probably indicates a number of issues: 1) they have been burned in the past by an employee who did not have the skills necessary to meet the job requirements; 2) they do not have the time to waste on candidates who do not meet certain qualifications; or, 3) there have been legal issues surrounding past hiring practices and the company does not want to run the risk of being sued.

Whatever the case, the company is letting applicants know that they only want those who meet their requirements to apply. If you know that you do not meet the minimum qualifications don't waste your time applying for the position and move on to a position where you do meet the minimum qualifications. This is also true if you have to stretch your qualifications too much to fit into the job. If you are unsure whether or not you meet the minimum qualifications your time would be better spent applying for a job where you are absolutely sure that you meet all the minimum qualifications.

In most cases you have a pretty good idea whether or not you meet the minimum qualifications; however, what if you have cross-over skills like knowing Word for the PC for a job requiring Word on a Mac? Should you apply anyway? Perhaps, but only if you are confident that there is a small learning curve in meeting the minimum qualification. And, this should be communicated to the employer in your cover letter or email.

To make this point, let's say that a company is hiring for an Administrative Assistant for an accounting firm and you have a Ph.D. in microbiology and have worked as a Research Assistant for a university. Should you apply anyway? With the glut of applicants in the job market, employers today are looking for candidates with more relevant work experience. Your first order of business would be to limit your job search to those positions that directly relate to your formal training or work history.

Secondly, if you do apply for positions where you might have to stretch your qualifications a bit, help the employer by explaining to him or her how your skills are transferable to the duties they need you to perform. The more you have to stretch yourself for the position you are applying for the more work you have to do to sell the employer on how relevant your qualifications are for the position. In this example the Ph.D. could spend a lot of time trying to convince the accounting company that they should hire him as an Administrative Assistant, or he could better use the time to look for other Research Assistant positions. If no Research Assistant jobs are available, another option maybe to enroll in an Administrative Assistant training and then begin looking for a job in that field.

In times past applicants would send in their resumes assuming that if they did not meet the minimum qualifications their resume could be forwarded to someone else who might need their skills. Today, this is not as effective as before because employers are under a lot of pressure to fill a need quickly so they normally don't take the time to cross-check a resume with other open positions in the company, even in larger companies with a Human Resource department.

So do a checklist first of the minimum qualifications to see if there is a match. The more matches you find where you meet all the minimum qualifications, the more opportunities you will have to move *From Resume to Work*.

5. Not Being Present

Employers *always* want to know what you are doing right now. If your resume does not have a "Present" date on it, the employer is left with their own assumptions about you, and compared to the resume that explains what the applicant is doing currently, the "un-Present" resume is usually passed over.

Having "Present" on your resume is like having an unspoken job reference. Sad, but true, the employer's mantra is, "If no one else wants you, why should I want you?" If a resume shows that someone has been out of work for an extended period of time and is not currently doing anything relevant to further their career, this sends up a red flag. In the employer's mind they are thinking, "If you are so good, then why don't you already have a job?" They want to know what the problem really is—perhaps you are flaky or stressed or lazy or unreliable, they may think. In any case, there is more of an uphill battle for connecting with the employer if the resume does not explain what the person is presently doing.

In an article entitled, *Companies won't even look at resumes of the long-term unemployed* (go to **/FRTW52**), Brad Plumer makes this observation:

> Matthew O'Brien reports on a striking recent experiment by Rand Ghayad of Northeastern University. He sent out 4,800 fake resumes at random for 600 job openings. And what he found is that employers would rather call back someone with *no* relevant experience who's only been out of work for a few months than someone with more relevant experience who's been out of work for longer than six months.

> In other words, it doesn't matter how much experience you have. It doesn't matter why you lost your previous job — it could have been bad luck. If you've been out of work for more than six months, you're essentially unemployable. Many companies won't even consider you for a job.

It becomes extremely important to send a signal to the employer that you are a desirable candidate currently active in the job market. In my next section, **You Must Be Present**, you are given four strategies on how to update your resume so that you can use the word *Present*. Remember, this simple word sends a signal to the employer that you are an active participant in the job market.

Rejected Anyway

As stated before, no one likes rejection, especially when it comes to their resume. Unfortunately, even if you avoid all of the pitfalls stated in this section your resume may be rejected anyway.

Why? Because there may be other reasons which may not be easily identifiable and that you can do little or nothing about. These include:

a) The employer has already pre-selected a candidate and is going through the job search motion to satisfy human resources or other legal requirements.
b) The employer has a personal bias against your name, address, school, reference, past employer, background information, social media posts, etc.
c) The employer already knows you and does not plan to hire you for whatever reason.
d) The employer plans to keep the position vacant but still has to go through the job search process.

Every applicant comes up against being rejected anyway, whether they know it or not. In cases like these you have to remember to never get stuck on what you think may be the ideal job. You have to apply, follow up, and move on. It's the best strategy that will help you keep going and move you *From Resume to Work*.

Resumes That Get Rejected Checklist

Point 1: Always follow the instructions given on a job posting, especially in the *How To Apply* section.

Point 2: Look for challenges in your own resume and enlist the help of others to eliminate these challenges.

Point 3: Don't assume that your resume is perfect. Get another set of eyes to help you from being careless on it.

Point 4: Make it a habit of applying to jobs where you know you meet the minimum qualifications. Avoid those positions where you have to stretch your experience to meet minimum qualifications.

Point 5: Always show on your resume what you are presently doing.

Point 6: Following all these points is not a cure-all for your resume being rejected, so stay encouraged and keep pressing forward.

You Must Be Present

Your resume literally has seconds to make a first impression on the employer, so what you don't want to do is to leave the employer with more questions about you than answers.

One question on the employer's mind is *what are you doing now?* They want to know why you are applying for their job. If you are transitioning from a current job then what job are you transitioning from? If you are going to school, then what are you learning and how is it going to benefit them? If you are in your own business, what business are you in and how is it relevant to the position you are applying for now? If you are not working, in school, or in your own business, what are you doing to keep yourself up-to-date in the changing job market?

You must answer these questions so the reviewer can scan through your resume without hesitation and without doing a doubtful double-take.

When you list a job or school or business that you are presently involved in it helps keep your resume at the top of the applicant stack. In this section we will look at four ways that you can make sure that the employer knows that you and your resume are present and accounted for:

1. Present with a job.
2. Present with education or training.
3. Present in your own business.
4. Present as a volunteer.

1. Be Present With A Job

This point may seem confusing because you might be thinking that if you were present with a job then why would you need this advice in the first place? And how can you start looking for a job by having a job? The jobs that are described in this section are not necessarily your permanent, benefitted, long-term jobs; they are usually your stepping-stone jobs—a relevant job that you can use to build your resume in order to find the job that you want.

The illustration below shows a section of a resume that lists the applicant presently working for another company. Employers like to see this because it shows that the person applying for the position is employable. They also like to see it because they can get a recent job reference if needed. To them, if someone else is willing to hire you then they may be willing to hire you as well. So it is better to begin your search for your next job while you are in your current job.

Employment	**Wide World Importers**, *Newport, RI*	*2015 - Present*
	Customer Service Representative	
	• Work with 28 sales professionals covering 2 states (Rhode Island and Connecticut), responsible for more than 3,800 individual and corporate accounts.	
	• Support sales reps in opening new accounts and upgrading existing service.	
	• Quickly and effectively solve customer challenges.	
	• Maintain quality control/satisfaction records, constantly seeking new ways to improve customer service.	

But how can you be present if you are not working now? The first thing to do is to develop a mindset that you are going to find immediate, short-term employment that you will use as a spring board for your permanent job. Here are six things that you can start doing today:

a) *Sign up to work for a temporary agency.* A temporary agency is different from an employment agency. An employment agency helps you to find a job and a temporary agency helps you to find temporary working assignments right away, usually to fill in a need while a regular employee is unavailable or while the company is looking for a permanent employee.

In today's job market, employers see temporary employment as a valid job almost as much as regular employment.

You should sign up for a temporary agency. In fact, you should sign up to work for several agencies at a time because one agency might find work for you faster than another agency.

Working at a temporary agency is an excellent way to show your next employer that you are active in the job market. Do an internet search for temporary agencies in your area. I have listed several of them in the Resource section at the end of this book.

Find two or three of them in which you hit it off with the recruiter. For these agencies, you should develop a relationship with them by regularly checking in and sending them an update on what you are actively doing to supplant your skills for the job market. You could also let them know of jobs that you have applied for (that you didn't get) and put them in contact with the employer. This way you have an active relationship with the agency.

Because most temporary agencies conduct screenings and background checks, an employer knows that if you are listed with a temporary agency then your resume has already passed a vetting process and can be accepted at face value.

Therefore, as soon as you are registered with a temporary agency, put that information on your resume even if you are waiting for your first assignment as illustrated in the example below where as soon as Christopher registers with Robert Half International he places this information on his resume.

<table>
<tr><td></td><td></td><td>111 Waverly Place
Manhattan, N.Y. 10014</td><td>(646) 520-2613
chrisD@gnet.com</td></tr>
</table>

Christopher Donaldson

Objective
To obtain a challenging position within a Financial Institution that will allow me to use my management, sales & customer service skills to help grow the company.

Experience
2015–Present   **Robert Half, International**   New York, NY
Financial Manager

- Prepare financial statements, business activity reports, and forecasts.
- Monitor financial details to ensure that legal requirements are met.
- Analyze market trends to find opportunities for expansion or acquisitions.
- Review company financial reports and seek ways to reduce costs.
- Help management make financial decisions.
- Train employees on how to work with financial models.
- Review and enforce company policies and procedures.

2006–2014   **Dow Jones & Co.**   New York, NY
Regional Operations Manager

b) *Offer to do contract work or short-term employment.* This means that you create a time-specific employee relationship with a company to do a specific job for a specified (or indefinite) period of time. You often sign an agreement specifying that you are a contractor and not an employee; or, you sign an agreement stating that you are an employee for only a short period of time.

When you find contract work or short-term employment you work directly for the company. When you find work through a temporary agency (as described in Section 1a above) you normally work as an employee of that temporary agency.

Companies like contract work or short-term employment because they don't have to pay the enormous agency fees which could be 30% or more of the employee's annual salary.

One way to get contract work is to ask for it. For example, if you are on a job interview and you notice that the interviewer is a little rattled and his office looks disheveled and no one is answering the phones, why not simply offer to help him out on a contract basis until he finds a regular employee. You can organize papers and field calls until the position is filled. In many instances where a person filled a need by offering to do work through contract employment, that person ended up with a regular full-time job.

Search for "Independent Contractor Agreement" under Google Images for sample contracts. Bring one to the interview and if you see a need present the contract as your offer to temporarily help the employer.

Another way to get contract work is to utilize services that specialize in finding short-term employment. In the Resource section I have listed links to several short-term employment services as well as provided links for sample contracts that you could use with any employer.

c) *Accept day labor jobs.* Most people think of day labor jobs as manual jobs given to undocumented workers. This is far from the truth. Day labor jobs, oftentimes called "gigs," can be anything from modeling, teaching guitar, designing a web site, tutoring, house-sitting, working as a handyman, translating, cooking, bartending, telemarketing, writing, bookkeeping, painting, dancing, or repairing, just to name a few. These gigs last several hours, several days, or more. Many of them are listed on craigslist.org in the "gigs" section. A sample gig is below:

The key with day labor jobs is to, first of all, find one that fits your needs. Second, do the best job you can. And third, when the gig is done ask the employer if they would be a reference for you and if they would be willing to keep your contact information and place you on call. If they agree then you can add them to your resume as a present on-call employer. As an incentive you could say something like, "If you ever need help doing what I know how to do, call me, text me, or send me an email. I'll even give you the first hour free. I will check in with you periodically."

d) *Find a work-at-home job.* Work-at-home jobs are where you work for a company as an employee or as a contractor but you are telecommuting from home or from another undisclosed location. Examples of legitimate work-at-home jobs include working as a tax preparer for Jackson Hewitt, a sales person for the Chronicle newspaper, or a loan processor for Lending Tree. In each case you are working for a company but have the opportunity to work at home.

You can find work-at-home jobs by doing a Google search for "Work at home jobs" which will return thousands of search results. The problem with just doing a Google search is that not all work-at-home jobs are legitimate. Far too many are scams which require you to pay first with the empty promise of a legitimate job, or have you work under the assumption that you're going to get paid A when in fact you get paid B (or nothing at all), or ask you to do something which is illegal, like cash a bogus check.

Therefore, it is best to contact companies directly to ask them about their telecommuting positions. These positions don't typically require as much of a recruiting hurdle like a long application process and multiple interviews, and candidates can be working for a company in less than a week. One advantage of getting a work-at-home job is that once you find a job you can use this information to update your resume should you choose to do so.

According to Forbes magazine, the 20 most common work-at-home opportunities include:

- Account Executive/Manager
- Adjunct Faculty
- Bilingual Interpreter
- Case Manager
- Consultant
- Customer Service Representative
- Director of Business Development
- Engineer
- Graphic Designer
- Insurance Adjuster
- Marketing Manager
- Medical Coder
- Program/Project Manager
- Sales Representative
- SEO/Marketing Assistant
- Software Developer
- Systems Analyst
- Travel Counselor
- UI/UX Designer (Google it)
- Writer

In the Resource section of this book I have listed a number of legitimate companies offering work-at-home positions. When you contact a company be sure to search for jobs using the following key words: telecommute, remote, or work-at-home.

e) *Find an online job.* An online job for the purposes of this book is where you sign up with an online company to offer your skills to the online community. For example, Grant Smith signed up with Upwork (**www.Upwork.com**), an online company which connects enterprises, small businesses, and startups with talented people who can offer their skills online. Grant began offering his Excel, Access, and Macro Developer skills to the business community.

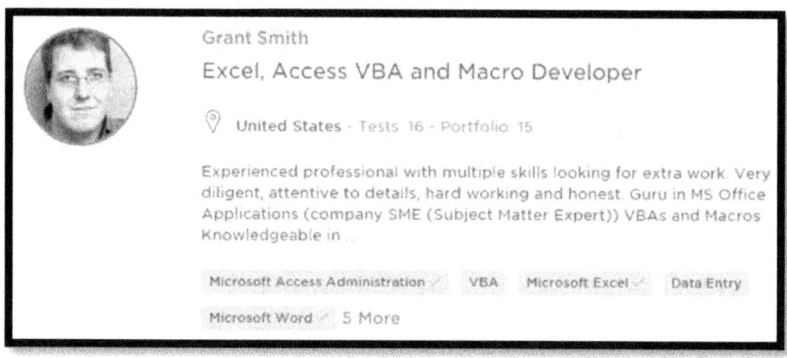

Once he signed up with Upwork he used this information to immediately update his resume to show that he was present with a job:

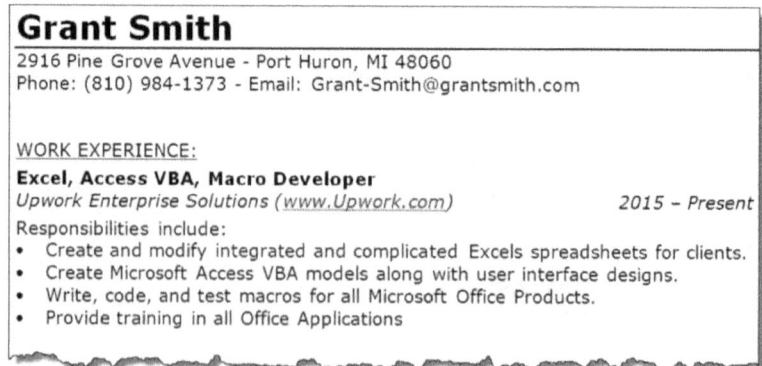

The benefit for Grant was that he could look for a permanent, full-time job while earning money in his field of expertise. (As of the date this book was published Grant billed 1,559 hours for Upwork. Let's see…his rate is $60.00 per hour, so multiply that by 1,559 hours and that equals not a bad income while looking for a permanent job.)

Finding an online job does not apply only to those with specialized skills because everyone at any skill level can sign up and then update their resume with the job information (see another Upwork example below).

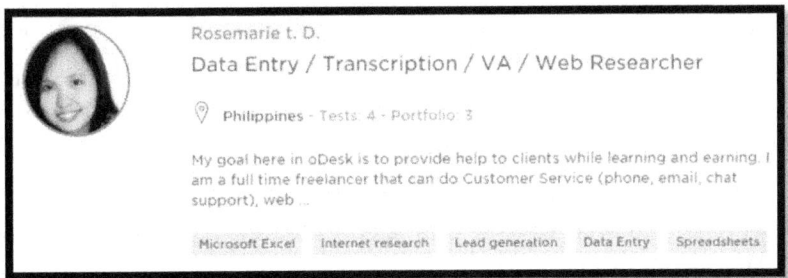

I have listed number of online companies in the Resource section of this book where you can sign up today and then update your resume so that you can be present in the job market.

f) *Get a job from family or friends.* You can offer to do a project for a family member or friend and then use that as a present job on your resume. It could be something as simple as organizing their files or cleaning out their garage or selling off household items for them.

In fact, one of my participants offered to clean out the garages of family and friends with the understanding that he would discard what nobody wanted and sell the other items on eBay.

When he started the project he updated his resume so that his current position read "Organizational Behavior Consultant."

After six weeks of organizing garages and closets and selling items on eBay he felt that he found a niche that he thoroughly enjoyed. A year later this has become his full-time job making more than double the amount of money as he would have made working for a company.

The goal of the strategies listed in this section is to get a job that you can quickly list on your resume as your present position. Be careful though how you list a current job if you only started there last week because you may come off as a job-hopper if your resume looks like you just got a job and are now looking for another.

When you apply for a permanent job you can let the interviewer know on the cover letter that you have accepted a temporary assignment while looking for more permanent employment with their company.

In the illustration at the beginning of this section which showed an excerpt of the employment area for someone working for Wide World Importers, no one looking at the resume would know that this person is in fact working under contract for a temporary agency. To the employer, this candidate is present—not with a temporary, contract, day labor, work-from-home, online, or family-friend job—but with a job.

2. Be Present With Education or Training

Another way to be present with the employer is to show them that you are currently involved with some type of education or training. This would include college, vocational training, certifications, online degrees or certificate programs, or other trainings in a specialized field.

Employers like seeing relevant education or training on the applicant's resume because it signals to them that: a) you can set and initiate goals; b) you have established a sense of purpose in your career; and, c) you have the ability to start and finish tasks (for those tasks you have completed).

> **Ninety-three percent of employers say they can be just as impressed with specialized certifications on resumes as they are with college degrees.**
>
> *GudeJob*

One caveat in using education and training on your resume is how much time and effort you are giving to your education or training and how relevant it is to the job you are applying for or the career path that you are on. If you are taking an online class once a week in basket weaving and you are applying for a job as a dental assistant, placing the basket weaving training on your resume might do more harm than good. It would be better, for example, to take an online class that is a part of a certificate program, thereby you could list the entire certificate program as your present occupation. In the illustration below Carolyn includes her current education which is both relevant to the career she is applying for and appears engaging enough to require her full-time effort.

Carolyn Gill

4096 Piedmont Ave. #347 Oakland, CA 94611
Home: (510) 555-1212 Cell: (510) 555-2112
carolyngill@mymail.com

Profile	Solid background in financial analysis and marketing, with strong emphasis in account management. Consistently exceed sales goals and customer service expectations. Experienced in handling international accounts and in presenting results of consortium operations. Skilled in developing and implementing standardized policies and procedures.

| **Education** | M.B.A. Marketing, Stanford University | *2015 - Present* |
| | B.S. Management, University of California, Berkeley | *May 2012* |

| **Career History** | **Gilead Management Group**, *Oakland, CA* | 2012-2014 |
| | *Corporate Account Manager* | |

The education or training that you list does not necessarily have to be some well-known university or national vocational or training program. It is just as acceptable to list training that you are receiving from individuals with certain skills.

For instance, you could list on your resume the training that you are receiving from someone who knows accounting, computers, car repair, or construction. You would simply list the training you are receiving and instead of listing an institution you would list the person (e.g., Internship Training by Bonnie Kwan, Certified QuickBooks Pro Advisor).

Below is an example of a resume where Alma lists computer training that she is presently receiving from her nephew. It is actually quite acceptable by employers to list education and training that you are taking from just about anyone who can help you improve your skills.

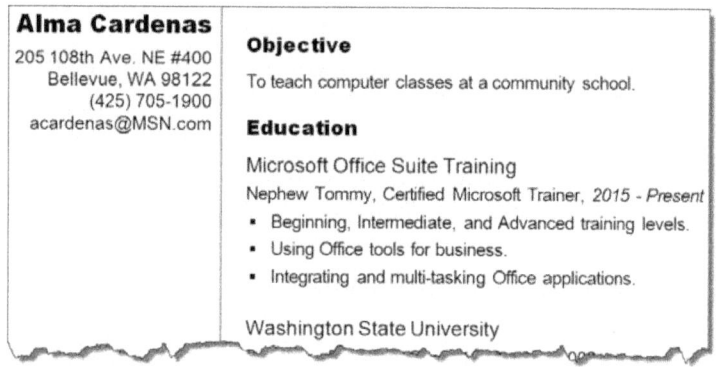

Alma Cardenas
205 108th Ave. NE #400
Bellevue, WA 98122
(425) 705-1900
acardenas@MSN.com

Objective

To teach computer classes at a community school.

Education

Microsoft Office Suite Training
Nephew Tommy, Certified Microsoft Trainer, *2015 - Present*
- Beginning, Intermediate, and Advanced training levels.
- Using Office tools for business.
- Integrating and multi-tasking Office applications.

Washington State University

In another brilliant example, one of my participants began taking online courses from *edX.org* (www.edx.org), a website which brings together classes from some of the top professors teaching at some of the best universities in the world. The courses are offered for free or for a nominal fee (as little as $25.00 as of this update), so Becky took Business courses from Harvard, Berkeley, and MIT and then listed them on her resume (see her education section below) while listing an online job as her present occupation as described in the previous section.

EDUCATION, SKILLS & TRAINING:

Business Certificate Program (www.edX.org)   2015 – Present

HARVARD UNIVERSITY
Leaders of Learning, *Professor Richard Elmore*
Understanding theories of learning and leadership. Gaining the tools to imagine and build
the future of learning.

UNIVERSITY OF CALIFORNIA, BERKELEY
Behavioral Economics in Action, *Professor Dilip Soman*
Principles and methods of behavioral economics to change behaviors, improve welfare,
and make better products and policy.

MASSACHUSETTS INSTITUTE OF TECHNOLOGY (MIT)
Supply Chain and Logistics Fundamentals, *Professor Chris Caplice*
An introduction to the fundamental concepts for logistics and supply chain management
from both analytical and practical perspectives.

San Francisco State University – *San Francisco, California*
Bachelor of Science in Business Administration, Major: Accounting   2006 - 2010

Becky only had to send out 12 resumes and within three weeks she had a full-time job. In her feedback several months later she told me that her boss who hired her graduated from the University of California Berkeley and was impressed that she was taking classes from his old alma mater.

Another participant was faced with a job announcement which stated in part, "Knowledge of Excel 2013 preferred." Elias had a solid background in Excel 2007 and felt that he met the minimum qualifications and had the experience to do each of the required tasks. He thought the job would be perfect, but the employer's preference for Excel 2013 bothered him so much so that he went to *Udemy* (www.udemy.com), an online learning marketplace offering over 32,000 on-demand courses that are taught by expert instructors.

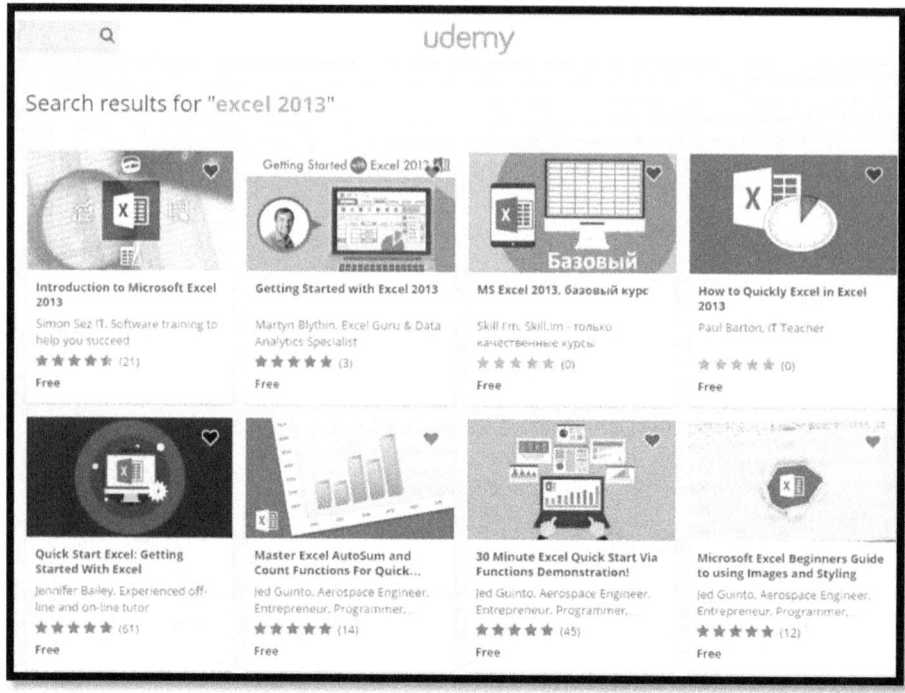

Search results for "excel 2013"

Introduction to Microsoft Excel 2013	Getting Started with Excel 2013	MS Excel 2013. базовый курс	How to Quickly Excel in Excel 2013
Simon Sez IT. Software training to help you succeed	Martyn Blythin. Excel Guru & Data Analytics Specialist	Skill I'm. SkillIm - только качественные курсы	Paul Barton, IT Teacher
★ ★ ★ ★ ☆ (21)	★ ★ ★ ★ ★ (3)	★ ★ ★ ★ ★ (0)	★ ★ ★ ★ ★ (0)
Free	Free	Free	Free

Quick Start Excel: Getting Started With Excel	Master Excel AutoSum and Count Functions For Quick...	30 Minute Excel Quick Start Via Functions Demonstration!	Microsoft Excel Beginners Guide to using Images and Styling
Jennifer Bailey. Experienced off-line and on-line tutor	Jed Guinto. Aerospace Engineer. Entrepreneur. Programmer.	Jed Guinto. Aerospace Engineer. Entrepreneur. Programmer.	Jed Guinto. Aerospace Engineer. Entrepreneur. Programmer.
★ ★ ★ ★ ★ (61)	★ ★ ★ ★ ★ (14)	★ ★ ★ ★ ★ (45)	★ ★ ★ ★ ★ (12)
Free	Free	Free	Free

Elias found the course he wanted, completed it in six hours, received a Certificate of Completion, added the certificate on his resume, and then included this excerpt in his cover letter when he applied for the job:

I also took to heart your need for an applicant to be knowledgeable in Excel 2013. Although I am already proficient in Excel, I recently received my Certificate of Completion for the course, *Microsoft Excel 2013 for Business Applications*, specifically to make sure that my Excel 2013 skills would be up to date in order to meet the tasks and challenges that you want me to complete for this position.

So online learning is an excellent tool to help you show your next employer that you are present in the job market. I have included a number of online learning websites in the Resources section at the end of this book. You can also do a Google search yourself and search for *free online education* or *free online training* or *free online certifications*. Be sure to add your particular industry information to your search (i.e., *free online bookkeeping training*).

The main point is that if you are involved in an education or training program that is both relevant and engaging, the employer will view this as your present occupation.

3. Be Present With Your Own Business

Using your own business on your resume is not only acceptable in today's market, but it is also commendable. Many employers want their employees to think outside the box and multi-task like an entrepreneur, so having your own business on your resume can show the potential employer that you are willing to take ownership for duties and responsibilities that they dish out. Remember, however, that this can be a double-edged sword in that you want the employer to be impressed with your skills but you don't want them to be leery that your passions lie elsewhere and that you could not be committed to their business. In the hiring process be sure to downplay your business aspects and focus on bringing the skills you have acquired into the new job.

Why would anyone use their own business on their resume? For a number of reasons actually, which would include the following:

Contracting positions: Some people who prefer hopping from job to job or working part of the year so they can pursue other interests for the other part of the year often use their own business to do contracting positions. Their business gives their resume the look of having seamless employment.

Consulting positions: Professionals who have a particular skill-set, like PhDs, paralegals, tax experts, technicians, bookkeepers, etc., often use their business on their resume in order to gain consulting work from individuals or companies. Having their business on their resume means that they don't have to explain gaps in their employment because they have "clients."

Changing careers: When someone has worked in one industry for a long time they can use their business on their resume to emphasize a different career they want to go into. For instance, when Erica wanted to quit practicing law and work for a restaurant, she established a business from her years of cooking for social functions and put the business on her resume. In short order she landed a job at an upscale restaurant.

Following up on a business concept: When people say to me, "I really want to start my own business," I often recommend that they to put their business concept on their resume. I then instruct them to begin sending out at least one resume each week and then tell them that they had better get their business concept together because when they get a call about their resume they will need to have their business in place. Each time one of my participants did this they reported to me that one of two things happened: 1) they felt a sense of urgency to get their business up and running, or 2) they stopped answering replies to their resume fearing that someone would ask them about their business they had not followed up on.

Reentering the workplace: When someone has been out of the workplace for quite some time, having their own business helps bridge the gap between their last job outside the home and their current job search.

Let me go a step further and say that I have discovered that for many people who say that they want to reenter the workforce their problem isn't reentering the workforce as much as it is realizing that they've never left it.

In some form or fashion most people don't realize that working for an outside company isn't the only definition of being in the workforce and many of the talents that they have developed were a result of experiences they have had outside the workplace.

For instance, Verna needed to go back to work after years of not being employed outside the home. Her resume started out looking like this:

Verna Gordon
37301 Oak Royal Road, Land of Oaks, CA 94506
Cell: (510) 465-0980
Vigi1050@aol.com

OBJECTIVE	To obtain a position where my selling, marketing and problem-solving strengths are used to help customers make quality decisions.
SKILLS PROFILE	I am detailed oriented and have over 20 years of successfully developing relationships that foster trust in my recommendations and loyalty to the company and products I represent.

EXPERIENCE

Publisher/Home Care Provider/Writer   2009 - 2015
Published a News Letter, cared for my mother in my home for six years (now deceased), and wrote a book.

Pre-marital and Couples Counselor   2006 - 2008
Allen Temple Baptist Church
Pre-marital and couples counseling

Salon Owner   1998 - 2006
Vigi Hair Clinic and Salon
Owned and operated a hair salon for men and women. Sold products, managed staff, payroll, purchasing, and advertising.

Account Manager   1986 - 1998
Xerox Corporation

Verna knew that she needed to be present with more relevant work experience to match her objective, so she took a personal inventory of her skills and realized that since closing her hair salon she designed, marketed and sold specialty pillows and pillow cases for women who wanted to keep up with their salon-styled hair. But because she did this off and on while caring for her mother she did not include these skills on her resume. This was a business that she owned and operated for years and was still something that she did on occasion. When this experience was included on her resume it was updated to the resume below:

Verna Gordon
37301 Oak Royal Road, Land of Oaks, CA 94506
Cell: (510) 465-0980
Vigi1050@aol.com

OBJECTIVE	To obtain a position where my selling, marketing and problem-solving strengths are used to help customers make quality decisions.
SKILLS PROFILE	I am detailed oriented and have over 20 years of successfully developing relationships that foster trust in my recommendations and loyalty to the company and products I represent.

EXPERIENCE

General Business Manager   2006 - Present
The Gilead Company
Designed and manufactured custom specialty pillows and pillow cases for a niche market in the hair care industry. Developed marketing strategies that including designing brochures and other collateral material, writing scripts for and producing television commercials, and attending trade shows to sell to retail customers. Sold products to end users through Ebay and other online channels. Managed the entire distribution process of the product including customer feedback. Also managed all administrative functions of the business including budgeting and accounting.

Salon Owner   1998 - 2006
Vigi Hair Clinic and Salon
Owned and operated a hair salon for men and women. Sold products, managed staff, payroll, purchasing, and advertising.

Account Manager   1986 - 1998
Xerox Corporation
Managed the copier needs of government and major

Notice that the updated resume utilized Verna's own business experience to tie in and enhance her objective on her resume. Take a personal inventory of your own skills by listing all the things that you have done for another person that has benefitted them in some way and that you have been compensated for. It just might be a business that you can add to your resume.

I also like Adele's story. After working for years as an advertising art director Adele followed her passion to write her own story about her and her friends trying to keep their virginity through college (*The V Society: The True Story of Rebel Virgin-Girls, /FRTW54*). She not only wanted to publish her book, but also wanted to help other writers publish theirs, and was a catalyst for me to publish my books.

As Adele pursued her publishing career she needed to earn a living so after doing an assessment of her skills, talents, passions, and goals, she decided to launch her business, Brandora (**www.BrandoraCollective.com**).

Brandora

BUSINESS CONSULTING + BRANDING for ENTREPRENEURS, START-UPS and SMALL BUSINESSES.

Adele initially used her Brandora business on her resume to get small consulting jobs, but as her reputation grew so did the jobs, even to the point where today Brandora helps businesses of all sizes with their start-up, branding, marketing, social media, and other entrepreneurial needs.

I like Adele's story because it emphasizes the importance of doing a self-assessment before launching into any business, even if the business is for the purposes of updating your resume. What a business or entrepreneur self-assessment does is to get you to begin to think about who you are and what you have to offer the business world. It helps ignite your passion to do something which is meaningful to you and which can lead to a fulfilling life. An assessment can help put your current job or next job in perspective knowing that in the bigger-picture scheme of things a seemingly dead-end job is just a stepping stone towards your next career move.

I have therefore listed several Self-Assessment sites for starting your own business in the Resources section at the end of this book. Yes you can start your own business just to update your resume, but you should always prepare yourself to take your business to the next level.

If you decide that you do want to start your own business to include it on your resume *and* to make some extra money while you are looking for a full-time job *and* to see where your own business could possible take you but you don't know where to start, you can start by clinking on one of the links below to see the kinds of businesses you can start tomorrow for a very small investment (remember /FRTW55 means typing in http://bit.do/FRTW55).

- 50 Businesses You Can Start In Your Spare Time - /FRTW55
- 10 Legitimate Business Ideas You Can Start for Less Than $20 - /FRTW57
- Top 10 Easy-to-Start Businesses - /FRTW58

I recently posted an ad for an Office Support Staff person for a retail company that needed help developing their ecommerce business. For one of the requirements I stated, "Must have ecommerce experience such as buying and selling products on Amazon or eBay."

Ken Longacre, for example, started an eBay business (www.eBay.com) by going through the steps of setting up and account on eBay, learning about buying and selling, and then conducting several transactions. Within three days—and for less than $20.00—his business was up and running. He then updated his resume so that the employment section included his eBay business as illustrated below.

Marketing and Sales Manager   2015 - Present
North Coast Solutions

- Research products online to determine their profitability in the marketplace.
- Acquire products through various sources including wholesale distributors and other local markets.
- Develop ecommerce marketing strategy in order to maximize sales of products. This includes determining where and when to market the product.
- Utilize several distribution methods to determine the most efficient manner to get the product to the customer.
- Provide customer service to each customer purchasing products in order to maintain customer satisfaction and increase repeat business and additional sales.
- Managed the accounting of the marketing and sales of products.

Vacation Specialist   1998 - 2015
Penn State University

- Responsible for internal sales servi...

With his eBay skills listed above, Ken would be a viable candidate for the position I listed. Oftentimes people think that having your own business is a turnoff for the employer, but in today's job market employers know that those who have owned their own business bring a unique set of skills to the workplace that have been sharpened by the candidate's entrepreneurial experience.

In one survey 88% of employers say they respect eBay as a viable business, and applicants who have eBay on their resume are seen as having a viable skill.

*Gude*Job

In another example, Bushawn turned his activities in helping his community into a business and use the term "Consultant" in the **Experience** section on his functional resume to communicate with employers that he presently had skills related to his community relations career goals. Employers today often find that candidates with consulting experience are able to multi-task at a high level and welcome their resume. An excerpt of Bushawn's resume is illustrated below.

Career Goal	A community relations position.
Summary of Experience	**Organizational management skills** • Organized volunteers, secured corporate donations and planned fund-raising events to pay for construction of $2 million Boys' and Girls' Club facility. • Serve on board of directors for club, help develop policies and procedures, and coordinate annual fund-raising auction, which provides more than $6,500 for operational expenses. • Recruited to supervise annual fund and membership drive for local library, raising donations 35% and membership 20% in two years. • Served two terms as secretary/treasurer of Parent/Teacher Association and suggested new parent/teacher conference that increased parent classroom participation 35%. • Managed three-member staff at rehabilitation hospital and increased productivity 25% despite operational changes brought on by two new owners in five years. **Communication/marketing skills** • Work with local businesses and civic organizations to gain sponsors for 30 soccer, 40 basketball and 25 baseball teams. • Developed brochure to attract and retain club members and sponsors. • Handle publicity for local March of Dimes walk-a-thon, which has seen participation increase 35% and donations increase 40% over the last three years. • Handled three in-house, high-volume accounts for rehabilitation hospital, and helped develop long-term marketing plan that increased number of clients 25%.
Experience	**Community Relations Consultant**, BC & Associates *(2015-present)* **Local Publicity Chairman**, March of Dimes Walk-a-thon *(2014-present)*

If you are going to use your own business on your resume it is a good idea to legitimize it so that it will indeed be presented as a business that you are actually running. Legitimizing your business means you have a professional business name along with collateral material like business cards, brochures, and a website. You might even have a separate mailing address and phone number, although these are not mandatory.

In addition, legitimizing your business provides another reference check for the employer who could utilize your legitimate business as a verification of employment. Here are 10 keys to making sure that your business is legitimized:

1. *Prepare a business plan.* This could even be a 1-page plan that describes the mission of your business and how you plan on carrying out that mission.

2. *Establish your business identity* including physical address, phone number, fax number, email address, and website. Also decide if your address is going to be other than your home address.

3. *Create collateral material:* logo, business cards, and stationery. This helps you to remain mindful that you have a legitimate business.

4. *Formulate your business* by deciding what structure it is going to be—a Sole Proprietorship, Partnership, LLC, or Corporation. You can find out the differences between them by going **BizFilings.com**.

5. *Register your "Doing Business As" name* for the city and state that you are doing business in. This is often called a fictitious business name.

6. *Register for* an Employer Identification Number with the IRS (**/FRTW59**).

7. *Create a list of the professionals* associated with your business. This includes your business attorney, accountant, and insurance agent. You don't have to pay them anything to list them for your business.

8. *Open a business bank account.* You may need additional documentation in order to set up an account. It is always good practice to have a separate account for your business activities.

9. *Put your business on social media*, especially **Facebook**, **LinkedIn**, **Yelp**, and **Google**. You can add other social media as well. Then if the employer finds your business name through an internet search, it adds credibility to you as an applicant and acts somewhat as another reference check.

10. *Conduct a business transaction.* There is no better way to say to yourself and the world that you are ready for business than when you make your first sale or get your first client.

Legitimizing your own business may inspire you to look at running the business on a full-time basis.

Gude**Job**

Having your own business looks impressive and can do a lot of good for your resume. However, you must be careful not to rely on the owning-your-own-business aspect too heavily. If you appear to be a die-hard entrepreneur, red flags are sure to go up in the mind of the employer. He or she may want to know why you, the business-owning person, are applying for their job. *Is this temporary? Are you here for just a pay check? Is this just a stepping stone? Would you be too distracted with your own business to focus on my needs? Are you stressed out?* These might be some of the questions on the employer's mind.

To alleviate their fears, you may want to let the potential employer know that your business has helped you get to a certain point of success and acquire certain skills that you are now ready to use in a position that can offer you growth. In addition, you can say that you have tried the entrepreneurial aspect for a time and found you prefer working at a company where you can concentrate your skills in one area instead of spreading yourself thin over all areas of a business. The goal would be to let the employer see that you have already transitioned from self-employment to employment with a company.

Sharing this information would normally occur during the interview process since the employer may not be able to tell from your resume that you are in your own business. In fact, it is a good idea NOT to put "Owner" or "Business Owner" on your resume as the *present* position since you want the employer to focus on your skills rather than questions that would arise from seeing a business owner now applying for a job.

Also, if you tried running your own business but failed don't be concerned that the employer may think you're a failure because most employers believe that those who never failed never tried.

> **Over 90% of employers believe that those who had their own businesses but failed at it have nonetheless acquired a number of valuable skills.**
>
> *Gude***Job**

Understand that the employer wants to know what relevant skills you have presently that can benefit their business. So there are definite advantages in using the experiences from your own business to show the employer that you are present and that you are ready to move *From Resume to Work*.

4. Be Present As A Volunteer

There is a Catch 22 in today's job market—you can't get the job without experience, and how do you get the experience if you can't get a job? One answer is volunteering (see the study conducted by the Corporation for National and Community Service on volunteering entitled, *Volunteering as a Pathway to Employment Report*: **/FRTW60a**). Volunteering is usually associated with working for essentially no regular pay in exchange for experience or some other benefit and can occur in various settings including: a not-for-profit organization, an established for-profit business, or a startup company.

Before you discount volunteering note that a national study shows that by volunteering you can have a 27% better chance of getting a full-time paid job than if you don't.

See the insert below:

The Corporation for National and Community Service, a federal agency that promotes volunteerism, tracked more than 70,000 jobless people between 2002 and 2012 and found that those who volunteered had a 27% better chance of finding a job than those who didn't.

Why Volunteering Can Help You Get Hired

One reason, according to the authors of the study "Volunteering as a Pathway to Employment": acquiring skills or knowledge as a volunteer and then putting them to use may "demonstrate higher levels of capacity, potentially making the volunteer more attractive to and productive for employers."

Volunteering for a **not-for-profit organization** is traditionally what volunteerism is all about. When an organization lacks the human resources needed to fulfill a particular cause volunteers are the non-paid staff used to help support the mission. In a win-win situation the organization fills a position and the volunteer gets the experience.

When you want to add a not-for-profit to your resume as your present work experience you should find an organization that allows you to volunteer in your field. For example, if you have experience as an Administrative Assistant you can sign up through organizations like **VolunteerMatch.org** or simply do a search for volunteer opportunities in your area and specifically request positions that match your experience or interest.

I have listed a number of volunteer organizations and websites that can help you find regular employment in the Resources section at the end of this book.

Volunteering with a **for-profit business** is called an *internship* (or sometimes called an *externship*). Interns can receive no pay or they may receive a small stipend on a regular basis like paid employees or at the end of their internship period. The reason why some businesses hire interns is that interns can add value to the business by completing needed tasks, and the benefit to the intern is that they receive on-the-job training and the opportunity to apply for any open positions before they are advertised.

Over 86% of employers believe that volunteering can be just as demanding as regular jobs, especially since candidates receive no pay.

GudeJob

Most people think of internships as only summer opportunities for those in college, but a few savvy job-seekers are using internship strategies to find permanent jobs. Some strategies include:

a) Updating their resume to include a Career Objective as an Intern (or Extern) for a company that would help hone their skills.

b) Signing up for an online class and stating on their resume that they are seeking an internship where they can apply their training.

c) Specifically looking for internship opportunities online.

d) Contacting employers posting jobs and asking them for a temporary, part-time, non-paid internship.

In one case the employer posted a job for a bookkeeper when Sara, who had just completed reading *From Resume to Work*, sent in her resume with the words, "Experienced Bookkeeper Seeking Non-Paid Internship."

In her cover letter Sara stated that she was taking several Sleeter Group QuickBooks training seminars and wanted to intern in order to use her bookkeeping skills and the new material she was learning from these seminars. The employer was impressed by her request and called her in for an interview.

During the interview Sara brought an Internship Agreement which stated that she would work for 20 hours a week for 12 weeks after which she and the business would sit down and evaluate their relationship. The agreement stated that during the internship if the company wanted her to work more than 20 hours a week, Sara would be allowed to bill the business at a rate of $25.00 per hour for the additional hours worked.

Sara was hired as an intern and the part-time schedule allowed her the flexibility to not only look for other jobs, but also have a present job on her updated resume. After the 12-week period, however, Sara did such a great job as an intern that she was offered a job as the regular, full-time bookkeeper.

If you think you want to find an internship or externship opportunity as a pathway to updating your resume and finding a permanent job, be sure to check the Resource section at the end of this book where I have sites listed to seek out these opportunities.

Volunteering for a **startup company** is a bit trickier because these companies quite often don't have a track record and cannot offer the stability that an established business or not-for-profit can. According to the Small Business Administration one-third of new employer companies fail within two years, half will fail within five years, and more than two-thirds of new employer companies will fail within ten years (**www.sba.gov**).

Even with this risk, startup companies can offer volunteers a wide range of experiences and provide opportunities to grow the company from the ground up. Some volunteers may even be offered an equity stake in the company in return for their services, but this is usually offered to those who have a specific skill-set that the company needs. (There are many exceptions, however, like graffiti artist David Choe who received stock for painting the offices of Facebook which at the time was worth only several thousand dollars. David held onto the shares and when Facebook's stock went public David's shares were worth about $200 million.)

If you choose to volunteer for a startup company, you may want to develop the mindset that the job is simply an opportunity to develop your skills and springboard you to the next paying job. With that said, you still must keep a balanced perspective that when you work you want to do the best job you can because you never know what opportunities will become available.

The upside of volunteering for a startup company is that there are tons of them in every different field imaginable so that opportunities abound. The downside is that start-up companies have so many needs that they could bleed you dry and leave you feeling used. Before you volunteer for a start-up be sure to set your goals and boundaries (for example, only being available on Tuesdays and Thursdays), and interview the startup as a regular business would interview you.

Looking for a startup opportunity is not difficult. There are a number of websites such as **Startuphire** (<u>www.Startuphire.com</u>) or **Startupers** (<u>www.Startupers.com</u>) where you can view startup companies. Although these sites have a heavy bent towards tech jobs, it doesn't prevent you from contacting them to say that you are looking for a volunteer opportunity in your field, which could include work from administration to warehouse support and more.

Jeff, for example, took this strategy a step further. After going through *From Resume to Work* he began looking in local newspapers in the fictitious business name filing sections to get the name, address, and contact information of all types of startup companies that are required to publish their business information.

Jeff began sending companies his resume and cover letter stating that he wanted to volunteer for a startup company that could use his expertise. Within two weeks Jeff had three responses to his resume. He met with each company and selected the one he felt would sharpen his skills and offer him the flexibility to look for other opportunities should they arise outside the startup.

Jeff volunteered 30 hours a week and then used the volunteer job to update his resume as presently working. This landed him a part-time job that helped him make ends meet. Four months later the part-time job offered him a full time position and Jeff cut his volunteer time to 12 hours a week because he wanted to stay connected with the company believing that it had potential. A year later the startup received several substantial long-term contracts and offered Jeff a position for nearly twice the salary he was making at his regular job. Jeff jumped at the opportunity and has been with the company ever since. Today, the company is no longer a startup.

In the Resources section at the end of this book I list several sites where you can find startup companies to work for or offer your volunteer services. I have also listed strategies where you can find smaller, local startup listed in classified ads.

If you are working as a volunteer in any capacity, it is more than acceptable to add this information to your resume as you would any other job. In the resume section below, no one can tell that this job applicant is volunteering for a start-up company.

| Experience | **Assistant Programmer Analyst** | 2015 to present |
| | ***A. Datum Corporation***, Mt. Laurel, NJ | |

- Assistant to Lead Programmer on project to re-engineer sales order system.
- Designed and implemented systems utilizing EID and IVR enabling technologies.
- Worked closely with clients to establish problem specifications and system designs.
- Worked with Programmer Analyst to supervised two contract programmers.

Programmer Analyst   2010 - 2014
Fabrikam, Inc., Philadelphia, PA

The great thing about volunteering is that you can find opportunities that match your interests, experiences, or availability; and, as soon as you begin working you can update your resume to show your next employer that you are present.

Remember that if you are a star volunteer many organizations will try to carve out a paid position to keep you. Always take any volunteer position as seriously as you would a regular job. You may find a job there or use the position to get an enthusiastic recommendation for your next position.

You Must Be Present Checklist

Point 1: Your resume is more impressive to employers if you are presently working.

Point 2: Being present with education is more impressive to potential employers if you are enrolled in a relevant program that requires a majority of your time.

Point 3: Owning your own business will help you keep your resume skills up-to-date, but be careful not to not push your entrepreneurism on the employer.

Point 4: Becoming a volunteer is a great way to show the employer that you are active in the job market and can be just like having a regular job when applying for a permanent job.

COVER EVERY POINT

Question: When an employer receives your resume and cover letter, what key factor strongly compels them to pick up the phone or send you an email to ask you to come in for an interview?

Answer: Covering every point.

This section discusses the primary strategy for connecting your resume with the employer; that is, covering every point they make in the job announcement. The employment psychologists who train employers how to weed out applicants from their resume are the same people who strongly encourage employers to consider applicants who cover every point in the job posting. Therefore, if you want to absolutely increase your resume response rate you must cover every point the employer lists in the job announcement.

Employers have human resources needs and list their needs in job announcements in two main categories: qualifications and responsibilities. You cover every point by addressing every need in each category. The more you can say yes to each need, the more you compel the employer to respond to you.

When you cover every point the employer's response to call you in for an interview can be triggered by several factors:

a) The employer can easily identify that you have the skills and experience to do the job.

b) The employer is part of a hiring committee which scores resumes and because you leave no stone unturned your resume receives one of the top scores.

c) The employer is scared to death of being sued for not following the non-discriminatory legal requirements of finding the best qualified candidate for the job.

A study several years ago quoted employers as stating that less than 5% of job applicants responded to their job announcement by covering every point. This means that in most cases employers are left to face the often daunting task of finding out whether or not an applicant should be given an interview based solely upon their resume. I agree with this statistic because in my own experience from the thousands of resumes I have weeded through for jobs that I have posted it would be a good day if 2 or 3 for each 100 resume actually covered every point.

When you cover every point you have just made the employer's job of hiring you so much easier. You have actually given the employer some insight on the type of employee you could be for his or her company--one that can fulfill their human resources needs.

1. Cover Every Qualification

In order to cover every point to the employer's satisfaction start with the "Qualifications" section which is sometimes called "Minimum Qualifications" or "Required" section.

As stated in the *Resumes That Get Rejected* section, you should do a checklist of qualifications to see how many you can satisfy. Don't fool yourself into thinking that if you shine in one area but fail to meet the minimum qualifications in other areas the employer would simply average out the score and call you in for an interview anyway. This is simply not the case, especially in today's job market where there are often many applicants for every listed position. Stated plainly, do not take the minimum qualification requirements as a suggestion.

The employer has the qualifications listed for a reason so the first action taken after an initial cursory overview of your resume is to see if you meet ALL the minimum qualifications. If you clearly don't, do not waste the employer's time because he might remember you. If you are not sure and still want to apply, let the employer know why you believe your particular qualification meets all their minimum requirements.

How do you cover every qualification? You do this in four steps:

Step 1: Identify the qualifications on the job announcement. This may sound easy enough but employers sometimes use Qualifications, Requirements, Responsibilities, Skills, and Duties interchangeably. Qualifications are normally something that you need to have already to get the job. If an employer lists something that you will be doing or something that is preferred, it probably is not a true qualification.

Step 2: List the qualifications in the order they appear. (Not always but quite often they are listed by the employer in order of importance.)

Step 3: After each qualification write one sentence on why or how you meet that qualification. The reason why you write a sentence about each qualification is to personalize it for yourself as well as the employer.

Step 4: Remove the employer's qualification request leaving your list on how you cover every qualification. You can now use your list to connect with the employer.

To illustrate this strategy the figure below shows an excerpt of an actual job announcement for a Corporate Recruiter. The employer does not list a Qualifications section but rather states, "To be successful you will want to have:" which in essence is a Qualifications list.

To be successful you will want to have:
- Bachelor's degree in business or equivalent experience.
- 3-5 years of successful permanent recruiting for complex skill sets in a corporate setting.
- Strong interviewing skills and the ability to build rapport with candidates while gathering information for hiring decisions.
- Excellent written and verbal communication skills, articulate phone skills.
- Experience and high proficiency using Microsoft Office (Outlook, Word, and Excel).

When you've identified the qualifications keep them listed in the order that they appear. Again, it is not a guarantee that the qualifications are listed in the order of importance, but often times that is the case. Then write a sentence after the qualification on how or why you meet that qualification as illustrated below.

> **To be successful you will want to have:**
> - **Bachelor's degree in business or equivalent experience.**
>   I have a Bachelor's degree in Business Communication from San Jose State University.
> - **3-5 years of successful permanent recruiting for complex skill sets in a corporate setting.**
>   I have over six years experience of successfully recruiting professionals for a downtown corporate office and sales offices of a large corporation.
> - **Strong interviewing skills and the ability to build rapport with candidates while gathering information for hiring decisions.**
>   I organized over 200 interviewing committees where as the lead interviewer I maintained rapport with each candidate as I led them through the interviewing process.
> - **Excellent written and verbal communication skills, articulate phone skills.**
>   I utilized my excellent writing, verbal communication, and telephone skills to follow up with each candidate by phone, email, and other forms of written correspondence to let each candidate know their hiring status.
> - **Experience and high proficiency using Microsoft Office (Outlook, Word, and Excel).**
>   I utilized Outlook, Word, and Excel on an intermediate level, often providing instruction to my colleagues on various tips and trick to increase their efficiency with these tools.

Then remove the qualification requirements from the employer and use every point that you've covered in responding to the job announcement. And how do you respond to the employer's job announcement in order to make a connection? Here are seven ways that you connect with the employer when you cover every qualification:

1. **Qualification confidence.** The first hurdle that many job applicants know but don't share with the employer is that from all the applicants that respond to job announcements less than 10%

feel that they are fully qualified for the job. Most job seekers that I talk with believe you need to have a "fake it until you make it" attitude, but unfortunately for them employers are now armed with tougher interview questions and "working interviews" to weed out those trying to fake their way through the interview process. However, when you take the time to identify each qualification and then write down why or how you meet that qualification, you build confidence within yourself that you are qualified for the job and it is this confidence that connects with the employer.

2. **Easy reference on your resume.** You must always, always, always, make sure that the employer can reference each bullet point that you respond to in the qualifications section of the job announcement on your resume. This is a key point because it adds to your credibility as an applicant.

For example, in the first bullet point response above the job seeker refers to having a Bachelor's degree in Business Communication from San Jose State University. This information must correspond with what is on the resume like it is shown below. The employer should have no problem matching every qualification to what is documented on the applicant's resume. This makes a huge connection with the employer.

EDUCATION

Bachelor's Degree: Business Communication   2008
San Jose State University, San Jose, CA
GPA: 3.325 (Cum Laude)
- Member: Pi Mu Epsilon Professional Business Society (2004-2008)

PROFESSIONAL EXPERIENCE

HR Recruiter Specialist   2008 - 2015
Merchandising America, Inc., San Francisco, CA
- Organized over 200 interviewing committees to procure applicants.
- Successfully recruited 20% of top management who are still with the company.
- Trained 60% of HR staff on new HR software, saving the company $80K in training costs.

3. **Summary of Experience.** You can also connect with the employer by listing your responses to the qualifications in the Summary section of your resume (if you have one) as given below:

SUMMARY OF EXPERIENCE

A degreed professional with over six years recruiting experience as well as Lead Interviewer experience through each step of the hiring process. Skills set include excellent written and verbal communication skills and telephone skills. Additional skills include intermediate level experience using Microsoft Outlook, Word, and Excel.

4. **Cover Letter.** You can most definitely connect with the employer in your cover letter as illustrated below. Using bullet points to list your qualifications helps to ensure that you have covered every point.

April 7, 2015

Dear Prospective Employer:

I was excited to see your advertisement on Craiglist for a Corporate Recruiter because every qualification you ask for I have and more which includes the following points:

- I have a Bachelor's degree in Business Communication from San Jose State University.
- I have over six years experience of successfully recruiting professionals for a downtown corporate office and sales offices of a large multi-state corporation.
- I organized over 200 interviewing committees where as the lead interviewer I maintained rapport with each candidate as I led them through the interviewing process.
- I utilized my excellent writing, verbal communication, and telephone skills to follow up with each candidate by phone, email, and written correspondence to let each candidate know their hiring status.
- I utilized Outlook, Word, and Excel on an intermediate level, often providing instruction to my colleagues on various tips and trick to increase their efficiency with these tools.

I look forward to hearing from you soon. Thank you.

5. **Email Correspondence.** You can also connect with the employer as you email back and forth with him or her. Your initial email correspondence might look similar to your cover letter above, and in any follow up emails you would want to further connect with them by highlighting one or more points where you meet their qualification.

6. **Telephone interview.** Many employers conduct an initial telephone interview. This is a great opportunity to connect with the employer by responding to questions using your bullet point responses as to why you know you qualify for their job.

7. **Actual interview.** During mock interview workshops I tell students that they need to know what is on their resume because the employer is sure to ask them about it. And, if you know that your resume addresses all the qualifications the employer asks for then responding to interview questions is so much easier. You make the connection with the employer because what you have written and what you say are consistent.

Remember that your first goal is to make sure that you meet all qualifications in the job announcement. Then, you want to respond to each qualification and state why or how you meet that qualification. From this point you can use your responses to connect with the employer in a number of ways. After you cover every qualification, you are then ready to cover every responsibility.

2. Cover Every Responsibility

The responsibilities section of the job announcement is sometimes called "Duties" or "Job Description," and the purpose of this section is to give you an idea of your day-to-day activities at the company.

When you cover every *qualification* you can simply restate to the employer the qualification that you have; however, when you cover every *responsibility* it's best to give an example of how you can handle that responsibility. You do this in four steps:

Step 1: Identify the responsibilities on the job announcement by reviewing the entire job announcement looking for any reference to what you might be doing or what you might be responsible for at the company.

Step 2: Make a check list of all the responsibilities that you find (you can list them as bullet points initially as you did with the qualifications).

Step 3: After each responsibility give an example on how you have handled a responsibility similar to what the employer wants you to do. As much as possible, it is best to list each responsibility as a success you had in that area (i.e., "Earned Sales Person of the Month for selling $80K in merchandise during our slow season").

Step 4: Remove the employer's responsibilities leaving your own list giving examples of how you can do that responsibility. You can then use this list to make the connection with the employer.

To illustrate covering every responsibility the insert below comes from a section of an actual job announcement.

Executive Assistant for FUN Startup - $70K

Responsibilities:
- ✓ Manage executive travel and speaking engagements.
- ✓ Complete projects on time and with little supervision.
- ✓ Cheerily and tactfully manage non-private inbound inquiries to the CEO.
- ✓ Manage various executive correspondences, prudently sorting which to manage yourself or leave to the executive, and how to prioritize them.
- ✓ Be psychic. Proactively find ways to make the CEO's life easier by being observant and asking questions.
- ✓ Manage complex calendaring for all day-to-day business and personal activities.

Once you have identified the responsibilities it is always a good idea to keep them listed as they appear. After each responsibility write a sentence or two giving an example on how you have performed the same or similar responsibility or any success you have had doing that responsibility. This absolutely makes a connection with the employer. (In the illustration below your responsibilities would be in **bold**.)

✓ Manage executive travel and speaking engagements. As the Executive Assistant for the then-start-up, Optiks, one of the many hats I wore was the Event Planner where I was responsible for managing travel and other arrangements for all keynote speakers.

✓ Complete projects on time and with little supervision. As the Assistant to the COO at HAFCI I had a weekly project meeting where I had to report on the status of current projects and was assigned new projects.

✓ Cheerily and tactfully manage non-private inbound inquiries to the CEO. Since we operated multiple sites I had to manage inquiries from direct reports, senior staff, the media, and external stakeholders, often having to use my charm and wit to manage a range of personalities.

✓ Manage various executive correspondences, prudently sorting which to manage yourself or leave to the executive, and how to prioritize them. Each day I sorted through all non-confidential correspondence in the COO's physical in-box, and all general email correspondence and separated each into "Urgent," "Important," and "ASAP" categories, daily providing the status of each.

✓ Be psychic. Proactively find ways to make the CEO's life easier by being observant and asking questions. While at HAFCI I brought in the paper to the COO each day and read his horoscope to him. I am also a regular caller to the psychic hotline which helped me be proactive to the COO's needs.

✓ Manage complex calendaring for all day-to-day business and personal activities. I proficiently used Microsoft Outlook to manage the COO's business as well as his personal calendar.

Finally, remove the employer's responsibilities and use your points to connect with the employer. Here are three ways to connect with the employer when covering every responsibility:

1. **Confidence.** The first connection you make with the employer is the confidence you have in knowing that you can do the job. Employers can sense your level of confidence for being able to perform the duties and responsibilities they want.

For example, an HR Director and I recently interviewed for an Office Support position which would require some QuickBooks tasks. When I asked Alexis what she had done in QuickBooks she said she worked on it some with her mother and didn't elaborate any further. From her response I could tell she had no confidence in QuickBooks. What I was looking for—and what I didn't get— was a sense that she knew how to use the program. If she gave me even one specific example of how she used QuickBooks that would have shown me she had a higher confidence level than someone who had just "worked on it." Needless to say, Alexis wasn't hired.

2. **Correspondence.** Another connection you will be able to make with the employer once you have your responsibility points is that when you correspond with the employer—i.e., resume, cover letter, email, fax—you will be able to share specific tasks or other accomplishments that relate to tasks that the employer wants you to do. This is key is because every time you correspond with the employer in the back of their minds they are asking themselves if you can do the job. If you, say, have your responsibility points in your Summary section of your resume, this connects with them.

SUMMARY OF EXPEREINCE

Executive Assistant with over six years experience assisting upper management with event planning, travel arrangements, calendar prioritizing, project management, and other administrative duties. Proactive multi-tasking skills in being able to manage inquiries from direct reports, senior staff, the media, and external stakeholders while completing projects on time with little or no supervision.

PROFESSIONAL EXPERIENCE

Executive Assistant to the COO   2014 to present

HAFCI, San Francisco, California

· Assisted the Chief Operating Officer (COO) with all scheduling

---

Or you can use your responsibility points in your cover letter or email correspondence to connect with the employer as in the sample cover letter below:

Dear Prospective Employer:

I am responding to your ad for an Executive Assistant. I have experience working as Assistant to the Chief Operations Officer (COO) at an organization called HAFCI where we operated multiple sites and I managed inquiries from direct reports, senior staff, the media, and external stakeholders, often having to use my charm and wit to manage a range of personalities. I also had a weekly project meeting where I had to report on the status of current projects and was assigned new projects.

Each day I sorted through all non-confidential correspondence in the COO's physical in-box, and all general email correspondence and separated each into "Urgent," "Important," and "ASAP" categories, daily providing the COO with the status of each. While at HAFCI I brought in the paper to the COO each day and read his horoscope to him. I am also a regular caller to the psychic hotline which helped me be proactive to the COO's needs.

I proficiently used Microsoft Outlook to manage the COO's business as well as his personal calendar, and used Outlook for one of the many hats I wore as the Event Planner where I was responsible for managing travel and other arrangements for all keynote speakers.

My resume is included for your review and I hope to hear from you soon. Thank you for your time and consideration.

Sincerely,

Pat Applicant

---

3. **Communication.** Finally, to connect your responsibility points with the employer to get the job you must communicate to him or her during the interview process that you are the best candidate based upon what they want you to do. When you cover every responsibility you are able to show the employer how your skills align with the duties of the job.

Remember that employers want to know if you are the right person for the job. The more you connect your responsibility points with them the easier you can move *From Resume to Work*.

3. Cover Every Point

Some employment postings do not have applications sections neatly divided into Qualifications and Responsibilities and in these cases the postings are an assortment of qualifications, responsibilities, duties, skills, requirements, and minimums listed in no particular order. Job announcements like these are often posted by small businesses or companies without a Human Resource department. This is especially true when you see a job announcement where the qualifications and responsibilities are given in paragraph form and provide a less formal description of the work environment such as the example below of an actual job posting (I numbered each sentence for illustration):

THIS IS A PERMANENT EXPANSION OPPPORTUNITY

[1]We will be interviewing this Saturday so when responding please indicate if you are available to interview on Saturday. [2]For you regular ad-surfers who have seen this add before note that this will hopefully be the last day of interviews.

[3]Exceptional opportunity for a Tax Enrolled Agent/Full Charge Bookkeeper with 3+ years of relevant CPA FIRM experience (you will be doing mostly tax work with some bookkeeping work as we expand into more bookkeeping clients). [4]We always take a company paid three-day weekend in March and never work the Labor day weekend.

[5]You can expect to work about 100-150 hours of paid overtime a year spread out over our seven busy months of March through September. [6]Our boutique tax & financial planning CPA firm has concentrations in

entertainment, law, technology, small business, and other professionals. (7)We are looking to expand our bookkeeping services and this is where you come in.

(8)We are looking for someone who can take a shoe box and make financial statements out of it and get it into the tax software for a CPA to review. (9)You will be responsible for monthly bookkeeping/write up, payroll, city business tax, and more, for ongoing clients. (10)You will do start-to-finish tax returns for potential clients that are too small for our current CPA staff which we normally turn away.

(11)You will be trained in advanced tax preparation, client interaction, and client development. (12)You will need to be a self-starter with excellent interpersonal and communication skills. (13)Our long term goal will be that you continue to improve your professional skills and develop some of your own. (14)Success will bring great financial rewards.

(15)Our 11th floor, ocean view, smart casual dress code offices are in Brentwood. (16)You will receive four weeks' vacation (two office designated and two your choice), the usual holidays off, a complete benefits package including dental, and some of your compensation may be paid in a tax advantaged fashion if you qualify.

(17)We take two half-days a year after April and October, and devote them to a nice long elegant staff lunch with the rest of the day off after lunch. (18)The 59 year old principle CPA skis 20+ days a year and takes 6+ weeks of vacation a year and believes in treating staff as he would like to be treated himself.

[19]This is a permanent growth position where you will work hard and be well compensated for your success but still have time to have a balance in life and career.

[20]When responding put, "I have Tax & Bookkeeping Experience," in the title so we know you are not an Autobot as this has the potential to be a mutually beneficial relationship.

A job announcement like this may initially confuse you because the qualifications and responsibilities aren't easily identifiable, and for a CPA firm which has to be exact and calculating, whoever wrote this job announcement is probably a free-spirited person.

For an announcement like this you must resist the temptation to respond in kind (free spirited) and realize that at the end of the day every employer wants to know that they've been heard. Therefore, even for seemingly rambling job announcements you must cover every point. You do this in seven steps:

Step 1: Number each sentence. This may seem tedious at first but it will save you time and effort when covering every point.

Step 2: Categorize each sentence as a Qualification (Q) – what you need to get the job; Responsibility (R) – what you will do after you get the job; or, Something else (S) – what you may have to address that is not a Q or R.

Step 3: Group the sentences by Q, R, or S.

Step 4: Look at the Q's first. Make sure that you qualify for every Q listed. Then respond to each Q as you did when covering every qualification above.

Step 5: Next, look at all the R's and respond to them as you did when covering every responsibility above.

Step 6: Next, look at all the S's. Some of them may be information that you don't need or may require a specific course of action.

Step 7: Finally, translate your response in your email, cover letter, or resume as described earlier.

In the job announcement illustrated above I already assigned each sentence a number. The next step is to categorize each sentence as a Qualification (Q), Responsibility (R), or Something else (S) as given below:

(1) **Q:** If you are not able to make it on Saturday you cannot apply.

(2) **S:** This is just information the employer shares with applicants.

(3) **Q/R:** You must have 3+ years of relevant tax and bookkeeping experience to apply (Q), and you will be doing tax work with some bookkeeping (R).

(4) **S:** This is more information the employer shares with applicants.

(5) **Q:** You must be willing to work about 150 hours of paid overtime each year. If you cannot do it for whatever reason, don't apply.

(6) **R:** The employer mentions these areas of practice to let you know that this is the area you will work in as well.

(7) **R:** A part of your responsibilities is to help the firm expand their bookkeeping services in the areas just mentioned.

(8) **Q:** You must be a person who can take an accounting mess and organize it in a particular software program so a CPA can review it. In other words, if you are not detailed and organized and accurate, don't apply.

(9) **R:** This is a description of what you will be doing at the job.

(10) **R:** This is more description of what you will be doing at the job.

(11) **R:** This is description of what you will be doing at the job as far as training is concerned.

(12) **Q:** If you are not a self-starter or have excellent interpersonal and communication skills, don't apply.

(13) **R:** The employer wants you to be willing to develop and improve your professional skills.

(14) **R:** The employer wants someone who sees success as financial rewards.

(15) **R:** The employer is giving you a feel for the office environment that you need to be able to work in.

(16) **R:** You need to be flexible enough to accept the 2 weeks of vacation that they give you and not take vacation during the tax season.

(17) **R:** It is highly suggested that you participate in staff luncheons.

(18) **S:** This is more information the employer shares with applicants.

(19) **R:** The employer wants you to be a balanced person (but not during tax season).

(20) **S:** This is a critical sentence because it looks very much like one of those applicant tests that the employment psychologists want employers to use to weed out applicants. You are given specific instruction to put "I have Tax & Bookkeeping Experience" in the title of your email response. Not only should you put this text in the title of your email, but also make sure that it is exactly as it is written (even with the ampersand "&").

Next, after each sentence has been categorized group them by qualification, responsibility, and something else:

Q: Sentences 1, 3, 5, 8, 12
R: Sentences 3, 6, 7, 9, 10, 11, 13, 14, 15, 16, 17, 19
S: Sentences 2, 4, 18, 20

Next, look at all the qualifications (the Q's). You address these in the same manner as you did in the *Cover Every Qualification* section above by first making sure that you meet every qualification. If you don't, then move onto the next job announcement. Trust me when I say that employers appreciate applicants who apply that meet all the minimum qualification, and are annoyed with applicants who send in resumes that have vacancies in the qualifications section.

I recently re-posted a job announcement that I had posted six months earlier. When Teresa applied for the first job posting she did not meet the minimum qualifications for the job. When I saw her name again I assumed that since she didn't meet the qualifications before she most likely didn't meet them now so I rejected her resume. What if she had updated her skills so that now she met all the qualifications? Unfortunately for her she never got the chance to show me her new skills set (if they did exist) because she previously applied when she did not meet the minimum qualifications. You will do well to focus on applying for jobs where you know you meet the minimum qualifications.

In this case the Q's are identified as sentences 1, 3, 5, 8, and 12. In each of these sentences the employer is stating what you need to apply for the job—from being available to interview on Saturday to having excellent interpersonal and communication skills. The goal, and I say again like a broken record, is showing the employer that you are 100% qualified for the position.

Next, look at all the responsibilities (the R's) and respond to them as you did in the section, *Cover Every Responsibility* above. Remember that for responsibilities you want to give an example or a success story for every responsibility in order to show your future employer that you can do the job.

Don't take this task lightly. One of the keys to landing the job is when the employer gets excited about you, and a surefire way they can get excited about you is when you connect with them by relating your experiences and your successes to every point they make in the job announcement.

I was a part of a hiring committee for an Office Support Staff position and each one of us on the committee was responsible for asking Carlo a number of questions relating to the responsibility section of the job announcement. Carlo did his homework and was able to relate what he had done elsewhere to what we wanted him to do for our company. After the interview we could hardly contain our excitement. The next day we asked for his references and two days after that he was hired. To date, Carlo has lived up to his interview and has proven to be a great hire. Therefore, I encourage you to take the time to connect your skills, experiences, accomplishments, and successes to every responsibility listed on the job announcement.

In this case I have identified 12 responsibilities, or duties, or tasks that you will do in the job position—from doing tax work with some bookkeeping to balancing your work and non-work life except during tax season. Relating your past experiences with each responsibility places your resume at the top of the list. To connect with the employer, make sure that you address every responsibility.

After you have responded to each Q and R, the next step is to see if there is something else (the S's) that you need to do in order to be considered for the job. In this case there are four sentences that deal with something else. Sentences 2, 4, and 18 basically give you more information about the job announcement, but as stated before you need to pay attention to sentence 20 and do exactly as the instruction says. I have been in meetings with an HR Director who said, "This person's resume looks good but they didn't follow your little instructions to give a salary history so I'm not going to include them." And that person wasn't considered a candidate, all because they didn't follow my "little" instructions.

So, and again, don't take the instructions on how to apply as a suggestion. You could be getting your resume tossed for no good reason.

The last step in this process is to connect each Q and R (and S for that matter) with the employer through the seven areas mentioned above: (1) Confidence, (2) References on your resume,

(3) Summary of Experience, (4) Cover Letter, (5) Email correspondence, (6) Telephone interview, and (7) Actual interview.

For example, in the cover letter below I included responses to each Q and R from the job announcement. By doing so I have made a more compelling connection with the employer than I would have if I just sent a standard letter. Take a look:

RE: I have Tax & Bookkeeping Experience

Dear Prospective Employer:

I am very interested in this permanent expansion opportunity with your company that I read on craigslist and am available to interview with you on Saturday. I have over 10 years of tax and bookkeeping experience with Arthur Andersen where I annually put in over 180 hours of overtime, especially when I had to shred Enron documents. I am a self-starter with excellent interpersonal and communication skills which I have used to create QuickBooks quality financial statements for my managing CPA out of shoeboxes of client information. My additional accomplishments include:

- Assisting our firm to expand from 30 bookkeeping clients to over 1,500 in 4 years. Clients were in the areas of entertainment, law, technology, small business, as well as other professionals.
- Managing the bookkeeping, payroll, and tax-related issues on a monthly and annual basis for a majority of our clients that we normally would have farmed out to smaller firms.
- Completing 10 of the 12 steps of the annual post-Andersen former accountants training seminars, planning to finish the final two steps which would improve my professional development and further put me onto the coveted road of financial success.
- Participating in the Company Culture Management Review Team where we increased productivity by instituting an office culture of professional casual dress, quarterly staff power luncheons, vacation differentials, and guidelines for establishing a balanced work life.

My resume is attached for your review. I look forward to sharing skiing stories with the principle CPA. Thank you and have a very nice day.

Sincerely,

Pat Applicant

Remember to make sure that whatever you say on any correspondence such as this cover letter is consistent with everything else you say, such as on your email correspondence or telephone interview, and can be found on your resume and easily identified by the employer. In fact, the more areas that you can consistently respond to—cover letter, email, resume, interview, etc.—the greater the connection you make with the employer.

Okay, let me take a moment to review and summarize seven tips that I recommend you do for each job announcement based upon what I shared with you in this section. Following these tips will surely increase your resume response rate by connecting you with the employer.

Tip 1: Identify each qualification in the job announcement to make sure that you qualify for every one listed. If you do not qualify for every qualification then go to the next job announcement.

Tip 2: Write a sentence for each qualification stating how you meet that qualification. Most often qualifications are listed in an easily identifiable section of the announcement, but if they are not then you will need to read each sentence of the announcement to find the qualifications.

Tip 3: Identify each responsibility in the job announcement and write down an example of how you have completed the responsibility in the past or had a successful outcome fulfilling the responsibility. Keep your responses as short and as simple as possible. If the responsibilities are not listed plainly on the job announcement you will need to search for them.

Tip 4: Take each qualification and responsibility you have responded to and use this information for your resume points, Summary of Experiences section, cover letter, email correspondence, and interviews.

Tip 5: Do a "Fact Check" to make sure what you say in your cover letter, emails, and any other form of communication is consistent to what is on your resume.

Tip 6: Pay special attention to the "How to apply" section of the job announcement, making sure that you do everything this section asks you to do in order to apply for the job (well, within reason).

Tip 7: When you follow up with the job announcement be sure to remain consistent with your responses and continue to communicate the qualifications and responsibilities you have identified with the employer.

Don't Get Tempted

If the examples and exercises in this chapter seem like a lot of work in order to respond to job announcements, know that it is. But also know that it is the few who choose to understand and employ these strategies that rise above the rest and connect with the employer to get the interview that lands them the job.

Learning how to connect with the employer is like anything new you had to learn where at first it's difficult and time consuming—and perhaps you were tempted to give up—but as you press through the learning curve you will find that the newness wears off and soon enough you become good at responding to job announcements.

The same is true with these strategies in *From Resume to Work*. The more you employ these techniques—the second time, the fifth time, the twelfth time, etc.—the easier it will be to respond to each announcement. Therefore, don't get tempted to go back to responding to employers in ways that kept you unemployed.

If you find that translating job announcements into emails, cover letters, and your resume just isn't your thing, you can always ask for help. At some point in time everyone needs to ask for help. You can find help responding to job announcements at places like **Fiverr.com**, **VirtualCoworker.com**, **UpWork.com**, and the gigs section of **Craigslist.org**; and from $5.50 complete, or $6 per hour, someone would be willing to help you cover every point on the job announcement.

When you do get tempted to go back to your old ways refer to the study below conducted in 2012 and again in 2015 where we created a resume and cover letter for Pat Applicant who was looking for an Administrative Assistant position. Every Monday for six weeks we responded to job announcements on Craigslist spending 2-3 hours using the Blasting Method and 2-3 hours using the strategies in *From Resume to Work*. The results are given below:

Pat Applicant

Education: A.A. Degree
Experience: Six years
Skill Level: Intermediate Word, Excel, Outlook, Internet, etc.
Employers: Two
Present: Education

2012	Blasting	From Resume To Work
Duration	6 Mondays	6 Mondays
Hours Each Monday	2	2
Resumes Each Monday	35	5
Total Resumes Sent	210	30
Employer Connections	1	6
Resume Response Rate	.41%	20.0%

2015	Blasting	From Resume To Work
Duration	6 Mondays	6 Mondays
Hours Each Monday	3	3
Resumes Each Monday	50	5
Total Resumes Sent	300	30
Employer Connections	2	8
Resume Response Rate	.67%	26.67%

The results of our study for this book clearly show that it's not how many resumes you send but how you connect with the employer that will move you *From Resume to Work*. On another note, the Employer Connections received in our study under the Blasting method were for jobs on the lower end of the pay scale which did not match the Administrative Assistant position Pat Applicant desired.

In the next section you are given several checklists to help you before you get started. Take a few moments to go through the checklists before looking at your first job announcement in order to put these strategies into practice.

Covering Every Point Checklist

Point 1: Covering every point on the job announcement is the key to increasing your resume response rate.

Point 2: Make sure that you can meet each qualification before covering every point for qualifications.

Point 3: Respond to each qualification by writing one sentence on why you meet that qualification.

Point 4: Respond to each responsibility by giving an example of how you can handle that responsibility.

Point 5: If the job announcement does not have clear sections then group each sentence by qualification, responsibility, or some other task or information and then respond to each section as you would a qualification or responsibility.

Point 6: Responses can be listed as bullet points or in paragraph form.

Point 7: To maximize connecting with the employer it is best to put responses in as many communication points as you can.

CHECKLISTS BEFORE GETTING STARTED

At the beginning of one of my job information workshops I asked the 46 participants this question: "How many resumes do you think you can send out in a typical three-hour period?"

The responses shot back varying from twenty to sixty. I then asked, "How many responses from those resumes do you think you'd receive back from employers who actually want to interview you?"

The participants were a bit more sheepish as people confessed that they might receive one, but more often none. I then asked, "How would you like for me to show you how to take that same three-hour period and generate three or more responses to your resumes?"

Your Checklist Before Getting Started

I had their attention. I then began by giving them this checklist to review before they could make a connection with the employer and increase their resume response rate:

a) Understand that effectively connecting with the employer requires some time and effort in order to develop the skills before it can become second nature.

b) Start with a completed resume and cover letter and then use these as templates that will be tweaked for each job announcement that you respond to. If you are not comfortable tweaking your resume and cover letter, get a tweaker to help you.

c) Make sure that you have something that you are doing presently that you can show on your resume. Never send out a resume which essentially says you are doing nothing right now.

d) Take each step in responding to every qualification and responsibility without skipping a point just because you feel it doesn't apply to you.

e) Use the employer's own words as much as possible when responding to each qualification and responsibility. It's not plagiarism, it is speaking your employer's language.

f) Don't be afraid to sound redundant on your resume, email response, cover letter, and other modes of communication by covering the same point over and over. At least you'll be consistent.

Your Checklist For Each Job Announcement

I also shared this checklist that I wanted participants to use for each job announcement:

a) Do I meet all minimum qualifications? (If not, move on to the next job announcement.)

b) Write one sentence next to each qualification on why I meet that qualification.

c) Given an example next to each responsibility of how I can handle that responsibility.

d) Write a cover letter or email response using the responses to each qualification and responsibility.

e) Make sure that each qualification and responsibility that I mention on my cover letter or email response can be easily located on my resume.

f) Double-check to make sure that my resume and cover letter (or email response) are consistent.

Your Checklist For Staying Diligent

I then shared this information with participants: If you have ever seen an advertisement on how to make big money owning your own business, investing in real estate, or using the internet, what 99% of the ads don't tell you is this: in order to experience success you must put in the time and effort it takes to make it work; and, you have to stay diligent enough to keep working through your learning curve.

Similarly, increasing your resume response rate also requires diligence on your part, which includes:

a) Looking at your resume every week to see how you can make it less challenging to employers.

b) Resisting the temptation to blast your resume to employers especially where you clearly do not meet the minimum qualifications.

c) Spending more time with the job posting to completely respond to the qualifications and responsibilities listed by the employer.

At the end of the workshop I reminded the participants that those who were unwilling to remain diligent and apply what they learned would most likely be out of work far longer than those who did. I ended with this statement: "When comparing apples with apples, I have yet had anyone prove me wrong."

And now you have the strategies and tools you need to make the connection with the employer that is sure to increase your resume response rate. Now it's time for you to get started and to move *From Resume to Work*.

RESOURCES

The resources that I provide in this section are for reference only. I am not affiliated with any of the services listed below, and I personally cannot recommend them; however, I've included them either because my students have used them and found them useful or when I have asked user groups for recommendations for services these were the sites which were recommended most often. Always do your own due diligence before using any service. Also keep in mind that many of the resources listed below charge a fee even when they tell you that the information is free. For many of the resources I use an URL shortener from **http://bit.do**. This means that when you see a reference **/FRTW##**, you would go to the URL bar and type in **http://bit.do/FRTW##**. This saves you from having to type in the long URLs. If you are using this material online or through an Ebook, I have including links to many of them so that you can just click and go.

I would appreciate any feedback you have on any resource you use so that when I update this material I can continue to include or exclude services from this list. Feel free to send me an email at: **Edwin@FromResumeToWork.com**. Thank you.

Building Your Resume and Cover Letter

There are a number of places you can go to get resume and cover letter help and if you do a Google search you can find a number of sites which say that they offer free help to build your resume and cover letter. A number of my students have used them only to find out that you can build your resume and cover letter for free, but in order to print it or download it you have to pay a fee.

Even if you don't plan on paying for their services, going through the exercise of building your resume and cover letter may give you some tools to help you build your own resume and cover letter.

- www.resume.com
- www.resumetemplates.com
- www.resume-now.com
- www.resumehelp.com
- www.resumebuilder.org
- www.super-resume.com
- www.resumegenius.com
- www.gotresumebuilder.com
- www.mypdfresume.com
- www.e-resumebuilder.com

The resource below is a government-based service which contains a wealth of free information on building your resume, writing cover letters, and surviving job interviews.

- http://www.careeronestop.org/ResumesInterviews/ResumesInterviews.aspx

Resume Writing Assistance

Where do you go if you need assistance getting your life boiled down to one piece of paper? Some of us may be good as giving tons of information while others have no idea what to say. The resources below are for services that will engage with you, usually for a fee, in order to help you organize your thoughts onto paper.

It is not always easy trying to find assistance with writing your resume because if you cannot find help for free then you could spend anywhere from $5.50 to $150 or more. Here are 5 tips on how to find the right resume writing assistance for you:

1. Understand what you need. Take time to assess where you are in the resume writing process and what help you need. Are you starting from scratch? Are you updating your resume? What do you want your resume to say about you? What types of job or career are you going after that you want reflected on your resume? Take time first to ask yourself and then answer these questions before you engage with someone who will help you write your resume.

2. Learn something about the resume process for yourself. Before asking for help it is helpful to know something about building a resume. Check out some of the resources under Building Your Resume and Cover Letter to see what questions are asked and how the process works. You may discover that you are comfortable enough to do it yourself. At least you will know enough about the process so that if you do hire a resume writer the process would be that much smoother (and cheaper).

3. Evaluate their marketing. When searching for resume writing assistance take note of how the service markets itself. How does their website look? Do they have complimentary marketing tools such as a Facebook page, Twitter account, LinkedIn profile, or a blog? Although it is not necessary for a service to be entrenched like this to be able to offer good service, it has been my experience (well, the experience of my participants) that those services that market themselves well usually have a better pulse upon how to create resume for current hiring trends.

4. Ask to look at their samples. Ask the resume writing person to provide samples of resumes they have completed recently. Make sure that they are providing actual samples (the personal information can be hidden), and that the resumes are not templates (fill-in-the-blank resumes). If they hesitate one iota about providing you with samples then take my advice and move on to the next service. Anyone professionally providing a resume writing service should automatically know that they will have to show samples of their work. When you review samples take note of your first impression of each one. Look at the structure, formatting and word usage to see if it looks pleasing overall. Look for consistency in each sample, not the similarities (which may indicate that they are overusing a template).

5. Be clear on the cost, but don't haggle. A good place to start is to let them know what it is that you want them to deliver (for example, a well-formatted resume that highlights your nursing accomplishments that is created so that you apply for a job at

Kaiser Permanente). Make sure that the price quoted to you can do all that you ask; and, if necessary, keep asking questions until you understand what you are getting and what you are paying for. And, it is a good idea to get it all in writing (a simple email will do). But in the process of understanding what you are getting don't haggle over prices trying to get an exceeding amount more than what you are paying. You can ask for additional services but don't demand it. I've known instances where one of our job workshop participants continued to browbeat the resume writer for more services at the same negotiated cost that the participant ended up with a resume template full of errors. Although in most cases you get what you pay for, remember that it is most important to understand your relationship up front in order to keep the surprises to a minimum.

If you use any of the services below let me know and I might share your experiences when I update this material. Feel free to email me at: **Edwin@FromResumeToWork.com**. Thank you.

- Work Source (**/FRTW70**). A governmental agency offering free resume writing assistance and resources.
- How to Write a Resume (**/FRTW71**)
- **About Jobs:** Resume Writing and Job Search Assistance (**/FRTW72**)
- Susan Ireland's Resume Site (**/FRTW73**)
- Resume-2-Hire (**/FRTW248**)
- Resume Writing Service (**/FRTW74**)
- Resume Writers (**/FRTW75**)
- Grand Resumes (**/FRTW76**)
- The Resume Center (**/FRTW77**)
- Yelp (**/FRTW78**): (Just type in "Resume Writing Services" for your area.)

Here are some top Fiverr (starting at $5) gigs which participants have recommended were good resume writing services that have helped them put their resumes together:

- PhotosExpert: Will design a resume in PDF format (/FRTW79)
- Solutions_00: Will design a resume and a QR code for it (/FRTW80)
- The Backpacker: Will proofread and edit your resume (/FRTW81)
- Mrigaj: Will design, proofread, and edit your resume (/FRTW82)
- The Headhunter: Will write a professional resume (/FRTW83)

Temporary Agencies

Employment agencies help you find a permanent full-time or part-time job. Temporary agencies, on the other hand, help you find temporary work to fill in for a permanent employee who is temporarily unavailable or for a position which has not been filled.

Be sure to sign up for several staffing agencies but be careful not to sign up for too many because if an agency offers you positions and you continue to be unavailable then you will be dropped from their list. It is best to sign up for one and give it a week or two to see if they assign you to any positions, and if not then sign up for another agency but let the first agency know that you have signed up for another agency and will stay in contact with them regarding your availability. Be sure to stay in contact every week with each agency as to your status.

You can review a list of agencies by **going here** (**/FRTW249**), or you can start with the list below (in alphabetical order) all of which have been used by my participants with good success.

Elwood Staffing (**/FRTW85**): Offers temporary and contract employment in administrative, customer service, warehouse, automotive, oil & gas, construction, and skill trade fields.

Kelly Services (**/FRTW86**): Offers temporary and direct hire employment. Search thousands of contract, contract-to-hire, and full-time positions.

People Ready (**/FRTW87**): Currently dispatches approximately 350,000 workers annually to jobs in construction, manufacturing, hospitality, events, restoration, auto services, logistics and warehousing, retail support, waste and recycling, and more.

Link Staffing (**/FRTW88**): Offers temporary and full time employment services.

Personnel One (**/FRTW89**): A leader in temporary and direct hire employment.

Robert Half (**/FRTW90**): Offers temporary employment generally in the office and accounting fields as well as regular employment in many other fields.

Select Staffing (**/FRTW91**): Helps to find temporary jobs and provides job seeker resources.

Staffing Now (**/FRTW92**): A premier provider of recruitment and staffing services specializing in clerical and administrative jobs, as well as finance and accounting jobs, banking jobs and technology jobs.

Yellow Pages (**/FRTW93**): Go hear and type, "Temporary Agencies" in the **Find** section of the site for your area.

Yelp (**/FRTW94**): Go hear and type, "Temporary Agencies" in the **Find** section of the site for your area.

Contract Work and Short-Term Employment

With contract work and short-term employment you work directly for the company instead of working for an agency who has farmed you out to a company. The advantage of short-term employment is that it is far less expensive for the company to make the transition to hire you as a regular employee than if they had to hire you through the temporary agency.

Following is a list of short-term employment resources. Other than contacting each one directly and asking about their services, I have only a few references from participants who actually used this as a job strategy. Even so, that may mean that there is more opportunity to use short-term employment as a long-term job strategy.

Aerotek (**/FRTW95**): A temporary staffing agency that offers flexible staffing options.

Find the Right Job (**/FRTW96**): They require you to complete a profile and then show you a list of jobs in your area by zip code.

Indeed (**/FRTW97**): This site shows companies offering short-term jobs, from warehouse all the way up to a CEO. Participants I have talked with rave about this site.

Local Jobs Index (**/FRTW98**): They require you to complete a profile and you must put "Short-term" in the job description box.

Back Door Job (**/FRTW99**)s: This site lists domestic and international short-term jobs, some of which are outdoors and require travel to other parts of the world.

Career Builder (**/FRTW100**): This site lists many types of jobs, including companies seeking short-term employment.

The link below is a PDF download of employment contracts that several participants of mine actually used. A number of participants contacted businesses through the help-wanted section in local newspapers to offer their skills on a short-term basis. Two of my participants who found short-term employment this way said that although the short-term job did not become full-time, it did allow them to use it on their resume and eventually found full-time employment. Go to **http://www.gudejob.com/contracts** and click the link for the sample contracts.

100 Top Companies offering Work-at-home Jobs

Work-at-home jobs are best suited for those who have self-discipline and can manage their time well regardless of distractions. These types of jobs are great if you need a flexible work schedule or income while you are searching for a regular job outside the home.

The companies listed below come from a report listed by FlexJobs.com. When you click on any link below you are taken to the FlexJobs website where you are given a description of the company offering the work-at-home position. FlexJobs.com offers a subscription service where from $14.95 per month to $49.95 per year (as of the release of this update) you can use their service to help you find flexible jobs. Although those who have used them say their services can save you a lot of time and can help you find a job within a month. However, you don't necessarily need to use their services and can do your own research to connect with the companies yourself.

If you choose to sign up you will need to click the sign up link as shown below. You will then be taken to available jobs from that company. You can also search the website for job positions using the following key words: *telecommute*, *remote*, or *work-at-home*.

> sign up for FlexJobs today.

Most companies have you apply online and then follow up with a phone call. If you pass the initial screening they then perform a remote test on your computer to make sure that the system you use can handle remote tasks adequately. After that you are hired or placed in a queue of applicants to be hired. I have the top companies listed by our own rating and employment success rate of our workshop participants as of this update. The company links are below:

1. Teletech (**/FRTW101**)
2. Convergys (**/FRTW102**)
3. Sutherland Global Services (**/FRTW103**)
4. Amazon (**/FRTW104**)
5. Kelly Services (**/FRTW105**)
6. Kaplan (**/FRTW106a**)
7. First Data (**/FRTW107**)
8. IBM (**/FRTW108**)
9. SAP (**/FRTW109**)

10. Westat (**/FRTW110**)

11. UnitedHealth Group (**/FRTW111**)

12. Dell (**/FRTW112**)

13. Working Solutions (**/FRTW113**)

14. Intuit (**/FRTW114**)

15. US-Reports (**/FRTW115**)

16. Xerox (**/FRTW116**)

17. PAREXEL (**/FRTW117**)

18. Aetna (**/FRTW118**)

19. Humana (**/FRTW119**)

20. VMware (**/FRTW120**)

21. Salesforce (**/FRTW121**)

22. American Express (**/FRTW122**)

23. HD Supply (**/FRTW123**)

24. Forest Laboratories (now Allergan) (**/FRTW124**)

25. ADP (**/FRTW125**)

26. K12 Inc. (**/FRTW126**)

27. CyberCoders (**/FRTW127**)

28. U.S. Department of Transportation (**/FRTW128**)

29. Connections Academy (**/FRTW129**)

30. World Travel Holdings (**/FRTW130**)

31. About.com (**/FRTW131**)

32. Apple (**/FRTW132**)

33. U.S. Department of the Interior (**/FRTW133**)

34. Aon (**/FRTW134**)

35. Western Governors University (**/FRTW135**)

36. U.S. Department of Agriculture (**/FRTW136**)

37. Anthem, Inc. (formerly Wellpoint) (**/FRTW137**)

38. Pharmaceutical Product Development Inc. (**/FRTW138**)

39. Overland Solutions, Inc. (now EXL) (**/FRTW139**)

40. Appen (**/FRTW140**)

41. Covance (**/FRTW141**)

42. McKesson Corporation (**/FRTW142**)

43. Teradata Corporation (**/FRTW143**)

44. CACI International (**/FRTW144**)

45. Citizens Financial Group (**/FRTW145**)

46. Red Hat (**/FRTW146**)

47. Adobe Systems (**/FRTW147**)

48. Broadspire (now Crawford & Co) (**/FRTW148**)

49. Walden University (**/FRTW149**)

50. EMC (now a DELL company) (**/FRTW150**)

51. Infor (**/FRTW151**)

52. BCD Travel (**/FRTW152**)

53. Healthfirst (**/FRTW153**)

54. LanguageLine Solutions (**/FRTW154**)

55. Dell SecureWorks (**/FRTW155**)

56. Grand Canyon University (**/FRTW156**)

57. Precyse Solutions (now nThrive) (**/FRTW157**)

58. Real Staffing (**/FRTW158**)

59. University of Maryland University College (**/FRTW159**)

60. Symantec (**/FRTW160**)

61. AutoTrader.com (**/FRTW161**)

62. Sodexo (**/FRTW162**)

63. SuccessFactors (a SAP company) (**/FRTW163**)

64. Hartford Financial Services Group (**/FRTW164**)

65. Autodesk (**/FRTW165**)

66. American Heart Association (**/FRTW166**)

67. Nielsen (**/FRTW167**)

68. Ecolab (**/FRTW178**)

69. Erie Insurance Group (**/FRTW169**)

70. General Electric – GE (/FRTW170)

71. Edmentum (/FRTW171)

72. Polycom (/FRTW172)

73. Amerigroup (acquired by Anthem) (/FRTW173)

74. Health Net (/FRTW174)

75. ChamnessOnline (/FRTW175)

76. Kronos Incorporated (/FRTW176)

77. Teleflex (/FRTW177)

78. CVS Caremark (/FRTW178)

79. Thomson Reuters (/FRTW179)

80. GEISWriters.com (/FRTW180)

81. Canonical (/FRTW181)

82. Achieve Test Prep (/FRTW182)

83. Onyx Pharmaceuticals (/FRTW183)

84. Teach For America (/FRTW184)

85. Leidos (/FRTW185)

86. Unisys (/FRTW186)

87. BMC Software (/FRTW187)

88. Hanover Insurance Group (/FRTW188)

89. Perficient Inc. (/FRTW189)

90. Day & Zimmerman (/FRTW190)

91. Comprehend (/FRTW191a)

92. Pitney Bowes (/FRTW192)

93. 3M (/FRTW193)

94. Nationwide Insurance (/FRTW194)

95. New Teacher Project (/FRTW195)

96. MedAssets (now Vizient) (/FRTW196)

97. CenturyLink Technology Solutions (/FRTW197)

98. CIGNA (/FRTW198)

99. FlexProfessionals, LLC (/FRTW199)

100. **Magellan Health Services** (**/FRTW200**)

50 Companies where you can get an online job

The online jobs listed here are with companies that you can sign up for in order to offer your skill set to the online business community. What's great about this is that once you are set up (in most cases the same day) you can then add the job information onto your resume. What you need to be careful about is that you are rated and evaluated for each job you do and so your future employer would almost certainly check out your rating and use the feedback to determine your employment suitability for their company. So just don't sit on your online job, do something spectacular with it. The companies are listed below.

1. **99designs.com** – design

2. **Aquent.com** – design, marketing

3. **Arise.com** - general

4. **BrightenCommunications.com** – telemarketing jobs for everyone from teens paying $18.75 per hour.

5. **Clickworker.com** – online marketing, e-commerce, media, information and directory services, SEO content, translation, web research, data categorization and tagging

6. **CreativeGroup (RobertHalf.com)** – creative, interactive, design, marketing

7. **Crowdspring.com** – logo design, naming design, graphic design, web design

8. **Designcrowd.com** – design

9. **Elance.com** – general

10. **Fieldnation.com** – general

11. **Fiverr.com** – general

12. **Fourerr.com** – general

13. Freelance.com – general

14. Freelanceauction.com – programming, design

15. Freelancedesigners.com – web and graphic design, programming, photography, writing, fashion design, industrial design, video production, advertising, logo design

16. Freelanceindia.com – general

17. Freelance-info.fr – French, consulting; fee to join

18. Freelance-informatique.fr – French, general

19. Freelancemap.com – software development, web, system administrator, telecommunications & mobile, IT consulting, SAP, Management consulting, Engineering, Distribution, OLAP & Business Intelligence, Content and media, Service and Support

20. Freelancer.com – general

21. Freelancers.net – general

22. Gigblasters.com - general

23. Gigbucks.com - general

24. Guru.com – general, very popular

25. Helpcove.com – general

26. Hexidesign.com – Logo Design, Stationery Design, Business Card Design, Web Page Design, Banner Ad Design, Brochure Design, Poster Design, Flyer Design, T-shirt Design. Has Affiliate Program

27. Hoofdkraan.nl – Dutch, general

28. Hourly.com – general

29. ifreelance.com – proofreading, arts, data entry, graphic designing, photography, bookkeeping; fee to join

30. Jobboy.com - general

31. Joomlancers.com – everything related to the Joomla CMS

32. **Justanswer.com** - general

33. **Mediabistro.com** – writing/editing, production, graphic design, publishing; fee to join

34. **oDesk.com** (now Upwork.com)– general

35. **Peopleperhour.com** – programming, design, administrative tasks, accounting, PR

36. **Programmingbids.com** – programming, databases, graphic design; fee to join

37. **Project4hire.com** – programming, translation, consulting, graphic design

38. **Proz.com** – translation, interpreting

39. **Scribendi.com** – editing and proofreading

40. **SEOclerks.com** – SEO

41. **Taskcity.com** – programming

42. **TaskRabbit.com** – house cleaning, IKEA assembly, donation pickup, event help, office help, pet sitting

43. **Topcoder.com** – programming/development, graphic design, data science

44. **Trabajofreelance.com** – Spanish, general

45. **Translatorbase.com** – translator

46. **Tutor.com** - tutoring jobs

47. **Uline.com** – sales jobs

48. **Workhoppers.com** – general

49. **Xplace.com** – designing, programming, writing/editing, translating, marketing, photographing; fee to join

50. **Yunojuno.com** – general

Online Education and Training

Below is a list of online resources that you can use to only to enhance your resume and cover letters, but also to develop your personal skill set. I have only included courses where I received positive feedback from participants, or that the training is recognized by employers as some of the best they know about. I have limited the list to where you actually can find free courses or free certificate programs, but there are many others willing to charge you a fee if you want to do a Google search for them.

Academic Earth (**/FRTW201**) – Launched on the premise that everyone deserves access to a world-class education.

Alison (**/FRTW202**) – A five million-strong, global online learning community, filled with free, high-quality resources to help you develop essential, certified workplace skills.

Coursera (**/FRTW203**) – An education company that partners with the top universities and organizations in the world to offer courses online for anyone to take for free.

edX (**/FRTW204**) – An organization which brings together classes from some of the top professors teaching at some of the best universities in the world. The courses are offered for free or for a nominal fee (as little as $25.00 as of this update).

Free-Ed (**/FRTW205**) – Explore hundreds of free online courses. Some are very short, requiring only an evening or weekend to complete. Others are full one-year study programs.

Khan Academy (**/FRTW206**) – Offers practice exercises, instructional videos, and a personalized learning dashboard that empower learners to study at their own pace in and outside of the classroom.

Open Culture (**/FRTW207**) – Get 1100 free online courses from the world's leading universities — Stanford, Yale, MIT, Harvard, Berkeley, Oxford and more.

Open Yale (**/FRTW208**) – provides free and open access to a selection of introductory courses taught by distinguished teachers and scholars at Yale University.

Udemy (**/FRTW209**) – An online learning marketplace offering on-demand courses that are taught by expert instructors. There are free courses but many of them charge a fee.

Vocational Alliance (**/FRTW210**) – Helping students build a bridge between school, employment, and the adult world. We specialize in vocational training, but we also dabble in many other areas of learning and scholastic achievement.

Starting Your Own Business Self-Assessment Sites

For the purposes of this book many people will use the idea of starting their own business to update their resume—which is okay. However, starting your own business may lead into you deciding that being an entrepreneur is right up your alley.

The self-assessment exercises listed below are for you to begin to think about a career in your own business and isn't a guarantee that you will be successful or not, but rather are tools to help you identify where you might fall on the entrepreneurial spectrum.

I have learned that successful business owners come in all shapes and sizes. Being a successful business owner does not depend on one's education, background, race, handicap, label, social status, financial or economic challenges, or past mistakes. There is a place for anyone who truly desires to have their own business.

BDC (**/FRTW211**) – A banking site that has a good assessment questionnaire for entrepreneurs.

BizMove (**/FRTW212**) – Provides a quiz for whether or not you would be successful as an entrepreneur.

Entrepreneur Magazine Online (**/FRTW213**) – Good information for entrepreneurs along with a quiz.

One Stop Center (**/FRTW214**) – Site that helps you start, run, and manage your business.

QuintCareers (**/FRTW216**) – This site a number of career and job-hunting tests and quizzes to see how prepared you are for the job market or for your own business. I found many of the quizzes thought-provoking.

SBA (/FRTW217) – I like their statement, "Becoming an entrepreneur is not for everyone." Their test is to help you to see some of the hurdles that you will face if you decide to start your own business.

She Knows (/FRTW218) – A women's lifestyle site which asks if you should start your own business.

Self-Assessment Tool (/FRTW219) – This is a PDF with is more involved with the entrepreneurial self-assessment process.

Visual DNA (/FRTW220) – This has more personality quizzes rather than business start up quizzes but some of them are fun and interesting.

Volunteer Opportunities that could lead to a regular job

Volunteering can help you find regular employment by keeping you active in the job market. Through the volunteer activity you may find a regular position by connecting with the right people, or you could develop your skills to where employers want to hire you.

Whatever volunteer activity you do be sure to treat it as serious as you would any regular job because you never know how the activity can springboard you into a regular position.

AARP (/FRTW221) – Let AARP's Volunteer Wizard match your interests with great ways to give back. Answer a few simple questions, and the wizard will match your preferences with AARP volunteer opportunities.

Cool Works (/FRTW222) – Cool Works believes in the transformational power of seasonal and career Jobs In Great Places. As a niche job board, Cool Works' mission is to connect adventurous job seekers with employers and one another.

Forbes (/FRTW223) – 3 volunteer opportunities that will seriously boost your career.

LinkedIn (/FRTW224) – LinkedIn wants to help you connect with nonprofits that need you and your service.

The Peace Corps (**/FRTW225**) – The Peace Corps sends Americans abroad to tackle the most pressing needs of people around the world.

The Red Cross (**/FRTW226**) – The American Red Cross exists to provide compassionate care to those in need.

United Way (**/FRTW227**) – United Way's goal is to create long-lasting changes by addressing the underlying causes of the problems people face with education, income, and health.

Volunteer Match (**/FRTW229**) – We bring good people and good causes together.

Yelp (**/FRTW230**) – Type in "Volunteer Opportunities" in the Find search box for your area and Yelp will display organizations where you can volunteer.

Internships and externship opportunities

Although when you think of internships and externships people usually think there are jobs for high school and college students, many of these types of are offered to professionals and vocational job seekers as well. The sites below list opportunities for those seeking to apply practical work experience to formal education received.

Remember that the definition of "student" for purposes of Internships and Externships is anyone in the process of obtaining an education, even if it is from a vocational or trade school. This list below is only a sample of the many internship and externship opportunities available.

Bank of America (**/FRTW231**) – One of the nation's leading banks offers internships.

Internships (**/FRTW232**) – Internships.com is the place online where you're sure to find the position that's perfect for you.

Indeed (**/FRTW233**) – This site lists paid internships.

Look Sharp (**/FRTW234**) – Powered by Intern Match, Looksharp is the largest internship and entry-level jobs marketplace dedicated entirely to students and new grads.

Simply Hired (**/FRTW236**) – This site lists paid externships.

USA Jobs (**/FRTW237**) – This is a free web-based job board enabling federal job seekers access to thousands of job opportunities across hundreds of federal agencies and organizations, allowing agencies to meet their legal obligation of providing public notice for federal job opportunities.

Startup companies where you can find a job

Below is a list of sites where you can search startup companies in your area. Remember to have a clear objective when offering to work for a startup (i.e., if you offer to volunteer be specific about how many hours you will work and how long you will work them) because startups usually have so many needs that they can bleed you dry.

The other side of working for a startup is that they have so many opportunities available that you can get exposed to almost whatever you are looking to do in your career, and if you're lucky enough you could connect with a startup that could lead to a huge payday for you.

Angel List (**/FRTW238**) – Lists startups where you can browse jobs by location, role, market, technology, salary.

Startup Digest (**/FRTW239**) – The best ways to find non technical startup jobs is not through a job board but through networking. Go out and meet people at conferences, meetups, parties etc., through this site to find out about startup jobs.

Startup Hire (**/FRTW240**) – Our mission is to connect talented individuals to exciting career opportunities at startup companies and to accelerate the team building process for companies and their investors. These are some of the most rewarding careers on the planet, but they historically have been difficult to identify.

Startupers (**/FRTW241**) – Our mission is to help you land a job before you have an existential meltdown.

The Muse (**/FRTW242**) – Offering exciting job opportunities, expert advice, and a peek behind the scenes into fantastic companies and career paths.

Venture Loop (**/FRTW243**) – VentureLoop is the worldwide leader in job postings focused on venture-backed companies. Many of the job postings found on VentureLoop cannot be found on any other job board.

The list above is usually for startups in the technical sense— i.e., those which have received funding to offer a technical product or service. However, you can find startups in your local paper or online paper in the "Legal Notices" section where new businesses are required to file.

For example, from the Oakland Tribune I searched for "Legal Notices" and was linked to California Public Notices (**/FRTW244**) site where I searched "Fictitious Business Name" (or "Doing Business As" [DBA] in some other states) and got a list of new startup businesses. The list also gave me the name of the business owner and their mailing address. Once you have this information you can write the business owner asking for a job or a volunteer opportunity.

NEXT STEPS

At this point some have said, "Just get me to the interview and I'll take it from there." That's fine for them but what if you are one of the millions of people who are not that comfortable with the interviewing process?

In my follow up book, *The Hiring Committee*, I tell the story of when I walked a friend through the hiring committee process. It's a story, oftentimes very funny, where I reveal 12 secrets of the interviewing process that my friend needed to know in order to successfully navigate through the committee in order to get the job. Through this story I teach you the strategies as well. You can find out more about my follow-up book by going to www.TheHiringCommittee.com.

I also have another book entitled, *First Fired, Last Hired*, which is the third book in this series. I wrote this book as a result of my

time spent as a volunteer for a Job Information Workshop where we counseled thousands of people who were going through a job transition. What I discovered from the job seekers who came back through our workshops year after year after year is that they continued to commit the 40 sins of employment that kept them unemployment. In this book I share these with you and what you can do about it. You can find out more about this follow-up book by going to www.FirstFiredLastHired.com.

In addition, I have two very good resources to recommend to you today, both of which have received enough good feedback that I decided to become an affiliate, which means that if you purchase the product I will receive a referral commission.

The first resource I recommend is Bob Firestone's *The Ultimate Guide to Job Interview Answers*. This resource has been around for over 10 years and has been updated for 2015 with 177 answers to job interview questions. You can use the URL shortener (**/FRTW245**) to obtain all of the great interview information that this resource has to offer.

The next resource is a MUST SEE video on the job interviewing process. Jimmy's resource is called *Wow!...You're Hired!* and the video does a great job walking you through some of the pitfalls and challenges when you are faced with an interview. At the very least you should watch the free video information by using my URL shortener (**/FRTW246**). Unfortunately, runs on Explorer but not Chrome.

If you have any questions or comments you can always email me at **Edwin@FromResumeToWork.com**. Remember that you can also go to **www.FromResumeToWork.com** and enter in your email address in the email address space provided. I will then keep you updated on additional products from this series. Thank you.

THANK YOU

I would like to thank you again for purchasing this book. It is my hope and sincere desire that you will find it helpful and rewarding however you apply it.

I also wanted to remind you that by going to the book's website: **www.FromResumeToWork.com**, you can download your free gift, *5 Fixes to the Dangling Resume*, and sign up to get updates for other free gifts and promotions.

I also want to let you know that you can visit our blog **www.GudeJob.com** where colleagues and I share strategies and tips on how to find on the job success in many areas in life that we did not know we called jobs.

Now I'd like to ask you for a small favor. If you found this book helpful could you please take a moment or two and leave me a review for this book on Amazon? Just go to the URL shortener **http://bit.do/FRTW247**.

This feedback will help me continue to write the kind of books that will help you get results. I really appreciate it. Thank you and have a great day.

C. Edwin Gill